Perfected on the Farm:

A History of the Milking Machine in America

By Mike Gleason

Milking Can Be A LIGHT Chore Now!

PERFECTED ON THE FARM: A HISTORY OF THE MILKING MACHINE IN AMERICA

PUBLISHED BY

SEEDS AND SAWDUST MEDIA

Salt Lake City, Utah

ISBN 978-0-9853703-1-2

For additional copies, contact:

Seeds and Sawdust Media

1122 East Bueno Avenue

Salt Lake City, Utah 84102

(801) 635-4619

For educational use, volume discounts may be available- inquire for more details.

Our goal with this book is to celebrate the technological advances- modest as they may seem by today's standards- in the history of America's dairy farms. We hope to accomplish this by displaying advertisements, owner's manuals, and more of the era. We have gone to great lengths to credit the sources of these materials (see appendix). This book has been a labor of love from start to finish, and any inaccuracies or omissions will be addressed in future editions.

DEDICATION

I dedicate this book on vintage milking machines to my wife Janet. We have been together for 40+ years and she is the light of my life. Have we always been in total agreement in every phase of our marriage? No, but on the areas that really matter, Yes.

For the record, Janet has been the one who has found and purchased some of my more unique milking machines.

I would also like to give credit to Leland M. Houck, the farmer in Apulia, New York who hired a 14-year old boy and taught him many things about agriculture, and many other practical life lessons.

Thank you God!

Mike Gleason

Herkimer, New York

January 2012

TABLE OF CONTENTS

FOREWARD: WHY THE MILKING MACHINE CAME INTO BEING

By the turn of the 19th century, an unprecedented number of Americans were congregating in cities, as they do today, with no place in those crowded environs to grow the food they needed to survive. In comparison, agriculturalists- farmers- had plenty of land but a smaller labor force to produce the food to feed city dwellers. Milking machines were invented to help make farm chores easier and thereby ensure an adequate food supply all around.

As a kid working on a farm, I loved dairy cows. In fact, from early on in our marriage, my wife has said that I have milk running in my veins instead of blood. She also has always said that she expects to arrive home someday and find a cow in the cellar. Well, I promise there won't be a cow, but there might just be one more milking machine.

At the farm where I worked, they used the Surge brand milkers. Many farmers chose brands based on dealer availability and service. This particular farmer's uncle happened to be a Surge dealer and only lived three miles from the farm.

-MIKE GLEASON

INTRODUCTION

Why write a book about milking machines? Good question. One of the best reasons to write a book is because you are passionate about the subject, and I have never met anyone who is more excited about old milking equipment than my father Mike. He spent his working years in the dairy industry, and in retirement he devotes much of his time and energy to collecting old milkers and helping to preserve the rich heritage of dairy farming in upstate New York where he has always lived. He has amassed a large collection of milkers and related paraphenalia, including over 4,000 pages of advertisements, promotional literature, and operator's manuals that he displays at fairs and community events throughout the Northeast. It has been interesting to watch from the sidelines as his hobby has transformed from that of an enthusiast and collector to that of a true historian. For him, writing this book was basically just the next logical step in his quest to educate others on the important- and unappreciated- role that the milking machine has had on life in America in the 20th century.

As for myself, I am neither a lover of milkers nor a scholar by trade, so my own interest in this book is somewhat more general: basically, I see the literature that evolved to sell and support milkers in their day as a fascinating body of documents that reveals so much about our shared historical and cultural evolutions. By reading some of the old ads, you can see so much of our nation's own history mirrored back. For example, we no longer talk about "milk maids", but we used to- why was this? Well, at one point in time, women did a lot of the milking. Why was that? Well, it is probably not inaccurate to say that women did it because it was hard, dirty work, and the fact that men began to perform more of the milking chores when milking machines emerged and eliminated some of the drudgery is hardly a coincidence. This is probably an over-simplification, but it still makes you think, doesn't it? And this is just one example of the kind of thing that might jump out at you while perusing these pages.

In addition, I am personally of the opinion- and maybe I'm a little biased or even just plain wrong here- that, in popular culture and academia alike, the milking machine might just be the most overlooked technological innovation since the Civil War. While there are dozens (maybe hundreds) of books on the cotton gin, the sewing machine, and the steam engine, we haven't been able to find a whole lot written about the milking machine, and its impact on human civilization has arguably been just as profound as these other inventions. To help tell the story of the milker, Mike Gleason spent years digging through 150 years worth of archival material, and we have presented the cream of the crop in this book.

Whether you are a member of the dairy community or not, I think that this book should provide an interesting and at times amusing look back into our shared history. Enjoy!

Chris Gleason

Salt Lake City, Utah

April 2012

American Milker
Invented by L. O. Colvin in 1860
Cincinnatus, NY

COME AND SEE THE
AMERICAN COW MILKER.

PATENTED
MARCH 28, 1865.

SECURED IN
England, France, and Belgium.

A SURE CURE FOR

ACHING HANDS AND KICKING COWS.

Dates of American Patents secured by L. O. Colvin: May 22 and 29, 1860; Feb. 17, 1863; Jan. 14, 1864; and March 28, 1865.

We would respectfully call your attention to the practical utility of our NEW MACHINE FOR MILKING COWS, now being introduced for the first time in the New England States.

Farmers and Dairymen cannot fail to recognize at once, in this invention, the most important labor and time saving improvement ever offered for their use,—one which may, indeed, be ranked with the reaper, the mower, and the sewing machine,—the great inventions of the present day.

The success of the AMERICAN COW MILKER is only attributable to its transcendent merit. It is the result of years of study and experiment, the fruit of long and patient labor and large outlay of means, and could only have been carried to its completion by the consciousness of the incalculable value of such an invention.

☞ By this machine the four teats of the cow are milked at the same time; or, as each teat cup acts independently of the other, three-teated cows are milked as well as any, and cows giving more milk out of some teats than others does not interfere with the working of the machine, or "finishing" the cow.

☞ The operation is in perfect imitation of the natural sucking of the calf. Nothing could be more simple or better arranged for use. It is very small, compact, and durably made. It weighs only four pounds, and is easily worked. It is perfectly self-adjusting, will fit any cow, whether the teats are wide apart or close together, large or small.

A Company has been formed [THE AMERICAN COW MILKING MACHINE CO., 335 Broadway, New York City,] with an abundance of capital, and by new and improved machinery, Cow Milkers are now turned out with great facility and perfection, and those purchasing *territory* supplied with the Milkers at reasonable rates, if they do not wish to manufacture for themselves. Believing we have the best and most saleable labor-saving machine in the United States, we solicit the patronage of thorough-going enterprising men who are able and willing to become interested in the territory they wish to operate in.

Tell me, is old-fashioned milking
    Fully equal to the new?
If 'tis not, believe our story,
    We have something grand for you.
There's a *Milker* getting credit
    Every night and morning's dawn,
'Twas invented by one *Colvin*,
    And its name is *The American!*

See it once in operation,
    You'll appreciate it then,
For 'tis the best Milker ever
    Seen by women or by men.
Its construction so peculiar
    That it has great credit won,
And milking cow's but pleasant pastime
    When you use the *American!*

There was nothing came before it
    Was more useful or more grand,
And in this age of great invention
    It pre-eminent doth stand.
Farmers, will you go without one?
    When your friend, the Agent's gone,
And your cows come home for milking,
    You may think of the *American!*

Age of wonder and of science,
    Age which true inventors hail,
To thee is the world indebted,
    Now "there's no such word as fail!"
The *American Cow Milker* is selling rapid.
    Brighter hopes through each morning filter,
Every week there are *Five Thousand*
    Sold of the *American Cow Milker!*

At the following State Fairs and Agricultural Shows it was shown in the presence of thousands, in operation milking cows. Each Exhibition gave a special award and certificate of approval, signed by leading agricultural men after witnessing the working of the machine, viz:

NEW YORK STATE AGRICULTURAL SOCIETY, SARATOGA, *September*, 1866.

The American Cow Milking Machine Company, of 335 Broadway, New York, exhibit a Machine for Milking Cows, which is worthy of special notice.

H. G. DICKENSON, ⎫
J. G. PETERS, ⎬ *Committee.*
GEO. W. POLLEY, ⎭

American Milker
Invented by L. O. Colvin in 1860
Cincinnatus, NY

This early milker was extremely simple- no vacuum lines, no pumps, no pulsators. This simple device operated on "muscle power" alone. If you take the time to scan the text of the advertisement, which came out in 1866, you'll see a prosaic poem written about the glories of the new milker. It is worth a read: it promises a brighter future where science paves the way to success, and one can't help but consider how its patriotic tone (the milker actually was named *The American*!) must've sounded to a post-Civil War marketplace.

Anderson Milker

Manufactured Jamestown, NY
Late 1930's

SINGLE AND DOUBLE UNITS MILK TWO OR FOUR TEATS AT A TIME

Anderson Milker

Manufactured Jamestown, NY
Late 1930's

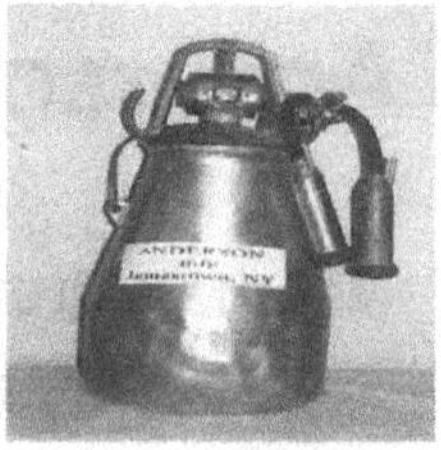

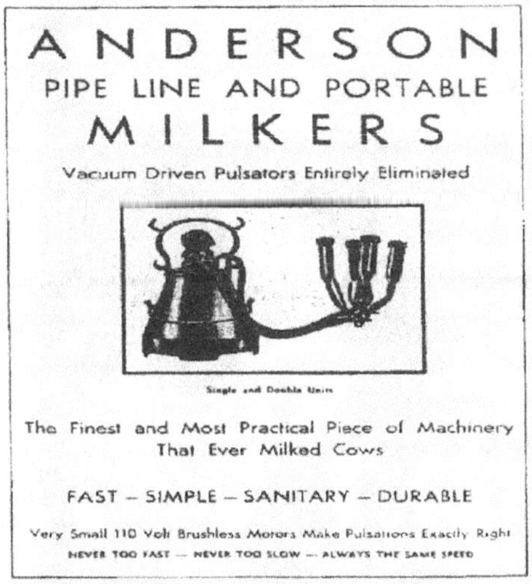

ANDERSON
PIPE LINE AND PORTABLE
MILKERS
Vacuum Driven Pulsators Entirely Eliminated

The Finest and Most Practical Piece of Machinery That Ever Milked Cows

FAST — SIMPLE — SANITARY — DURABLE

Very Small 110 Volt Brushless Motors Make Pulsations Exactly Right
NEVER TOO FAST — NEVER TOO SLOW — ALWAYS THE SAME SPEED

Single and Double Units.

ELECTRIC HEAD UNITS
FOR PIPE LINE MILKER OUTFITS

NO SPRINGS   NO SMALL HOLES
NO DIAPHRAGMS   NOT AFFECTED BY
NO ADJUSTMENTS   HEAT OR COLD

A very small 5 watt, 110 volt, brushless motor turns suction and pressure on and off in teat cups just as accurately as an electric clock - Never Too Fast - Never Too Slow - Always Just Right.

Operation

Electric Head Single Unit

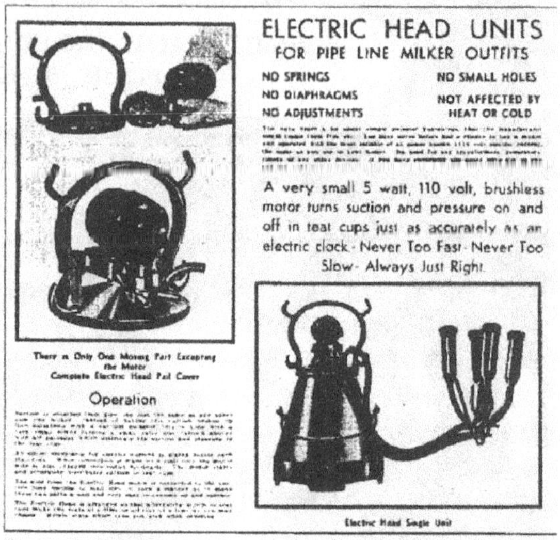

Electric Head Units.

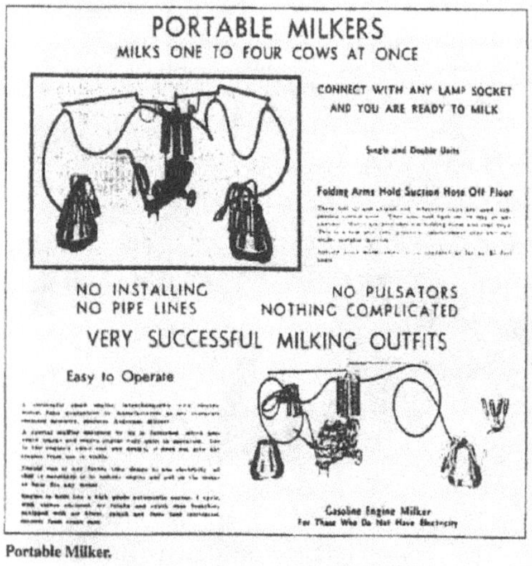

PORTABLE MILKERS
MILKS ONE TO FOUR COWS AT ONCE

CONNECT WITH ANY LAMP SOCKET AND YOU ARE READY TO MILK

Single and Double Units

Folding Arms Hold Suction Hose Off Floor

NO INSTALLING   NO PULSATORS
NO PIPE LINES   NOTHING COMPLICATED

VERY SUCCESSFUL MILKING OUTFITS

Easy to Operate

Gasoline Engine Milker
For Those Who Do Not Have Electricity

Portable Milker.

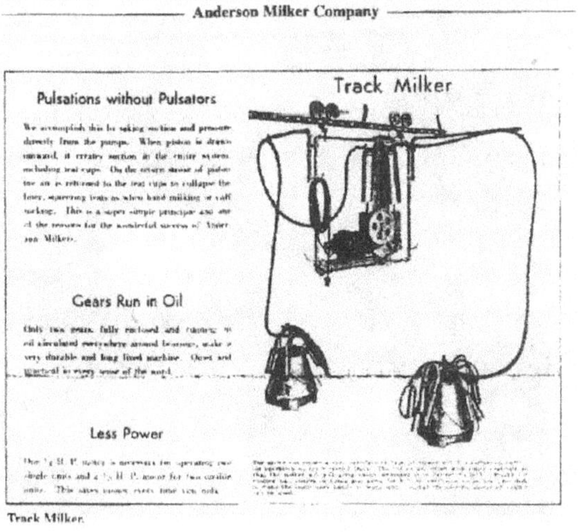

Anderson Milker Company

Pulsations without Pulsators

Track Milker

Gears Run in Oil

Less Power

Track Milker.

Baldwin, Anna

Anna Baldwin patented a device in 1878 that fit on a water pump. Anna Baldwin has to be credited with a pile of human ingenuity when she thought this up. Her device was never produced commercially, however.

The first patented suction type milking machine—actually a water pump with an arrangement for attaching it to the cow's teats. This patent was issued in 1878 to Anna Baldwin and was, of course, not commercially practical.

from DeLaval Milking Handbook

B.F. Berry & Co.

1315 2nd Avenue South, Minneapolis, MN.

Champion Cow Milker.

Ben Anderson Manufacturing Co.
Wisconsin, USA

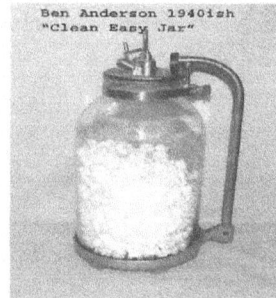

Ben Anderson 1940ish
"Clean Easy Jar"

This receptical jar is only Ben Anderson piece in Mike Gleason collection

advertisement from Ben H. Anderson Mfg. Co.

★ TRANSPARENT BAKELITE TEAT CUPS
★ "C-ALL" MOISTURE TRAPS
  Protects Vacuum Pumps
★ EASY-TO-CLEAN CLAW
★ FAMOUS SUPER VALVE
  Insures Fast, Uniform Milking
★ MILKS INTO ANY CONTAINER
  Shipping Can, Cream Set Cans,
  Glass Pails
★ REDUCTION GEAR RUNS IN OIL BATH
  Smooth Running—Quiet
★ GASOLINE OR ELECTRIC MOTOR POWER

Clean-Easy MILKERS

FASTER MILKING-LOW VACUUM-EASY CLEANING-SMOOTH MILKING ACTION

Illustrated above is the Clean-Easy Portable Milker, Model V1. A favorite with dairy farmers who prefer to milk into shipping cans instead of special containers. Model V1 is highly efficient because there is less to handle in actual milking, less to wash and keep sanitary. We can recommend this model for use in any dairy where milking into separate containers is not a requirement, where speed in milking, easy handling, and quick, positive sanitation is desired.

GLASS MILK PAILS
Glass pail equipment can be added to the shipping can model. They promote cleanliness—you can easily keep them as sparkling clean as your table glassware! What's more, you can see the milk flow into the pails, see and keep a record of each cow's milk production. Clean-Easy is the only milker to have modern, sanitary glass pails.

SUPER VALVE
The "heart" of the Clean-Easy Milker, the Transparent bakelite Super-Valve, has the same proven construction which has given sensational performance in over 25 years of service. The new POSITIVE ACTION SPRING of the famous Clean-Easy valve chamber insures positive vacuum and release without which successful mechanical milking is not possible.

CLEAN-EASY CLAW
The most sanitary claw on any milker today! There are no crevices or corners to hide bacteria—you can look through the claw from any opening—no hidden angles, curves, or threaded inside surfaces.

DESIGNED FOR EXTRA SANITATION
Sanitation has become increasingly important—and Clean-Easy Milkers are designed to make washing and sterilizing of milking equipment sure and safe—and at the same time save time and effort for the operator. It takes but a few minutes to thoroughly clean the Clean-Easy. All parts are easily accessible, no hidden surfaces to wash. You'll be amazed how quickly, easily and thoroughly the job can be done.

CONTROLLED VACUUM
Clean-Easy milks any cow—"tough" or "easy"! The controlled vacuum insures that you never get too much suction to injure the cow—yet always enough to do the best, most thorough milking job. Positive vacuum and release at every stroke of the pump.

BEN H. ANDERSON MFG. CO., MADISON 3, WISCONSIN

14

Ben Anderson 1938
Different styles of units.

First Convention of the
Ben H. Anderson Mfg Co.
April 5, 1938 — Madison, Wis.

S44A
Milking in Shipping Can

Ben Anderson Manufacturing Co.
Wisconsin, USA Patented 1938

Pictured below is a 10 gallon milk can receiver with vertical pistons. The 5 gallon glass jars that come with the Ben Anderson Milkers are beautifully embossed and can be found on occasion in antique shops.

And pictured below (far right) is a Glass Clean-Easy Milker with receiving jars and offset pistons.

Ben H. Anderson Manufacturing Company

Madison 3, Wisconsin. Clean–Easy Milker.

Pictured below is an early wooden framed shotgun can milker with electric motor bracket.

Paul Dettloff Collection, Arcadia, Wisconsin.

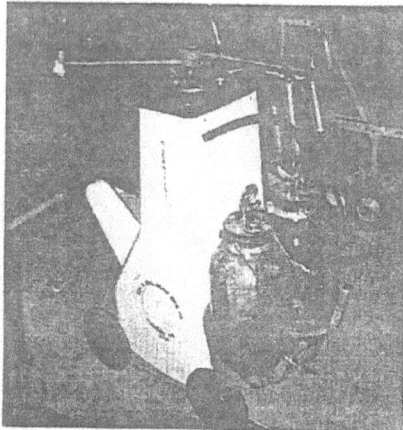

Paul Dettloff Collection, Arcadia, Wisconsin.

Paul Dettloff Collection, Arcadia, Wisconsin.

From Paul Dettloff Collection
Arcadia, Wisconson.

Blue RibbonElectric Milker
Mfg. by Electric Milker Corporation
Tower Building, Chigago, ILL.

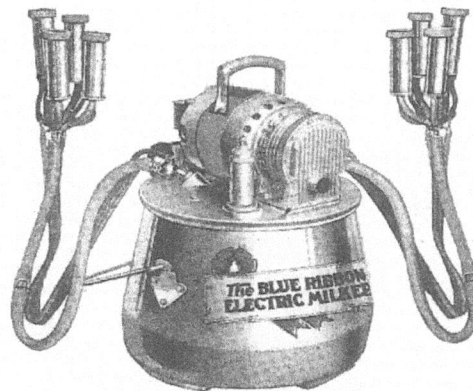

Caution

SOME milking machines have the pulsator or other parts mounted on the pail cover, and at a quick glance there is a slight resemblance to The Blue Ribbon Electric. Remember that The Blue Ribbon Electric Milker is the only one with The Complete Plant on the Pail Cover. Always look for the Blue Band around the motor.

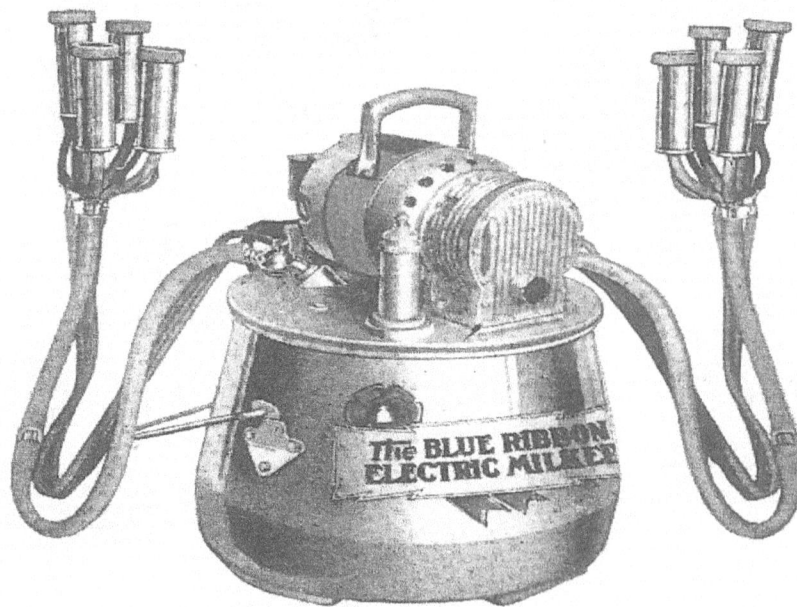

Electric Milker Corporation
Tower Building - Chicago

David Hamlin Burrell
1841-1919

Burrell B-L-K
1920

"It Milks the Cows Clean"

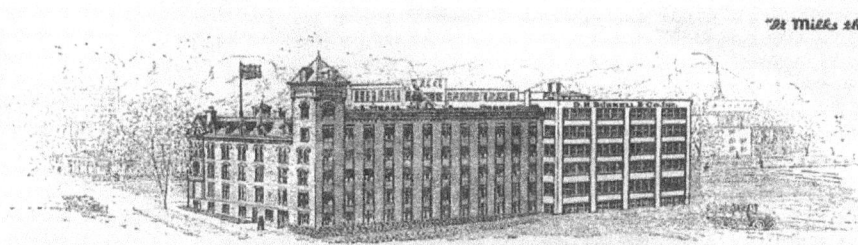

D. H. BURRELL & Co. Inc.

THE FACT that the Indians destroyed the settlement known as Little Falls, in the State of New York, in 1782, has no apparent relation to the business of D. H. Burrell & Co. Inc. today. Nevertheless, this historical fact serves the purpose of linking up the story of the Burrell family with the early days of American settlement and development.

Eight years after the Indians had wiped out this little settlement in the Mohawk Valley, a new settlement was started. And eleven years after that, one Jonathan Burrell, coming from western Massachusetts with his family, made his home at what is now the village of Salisbury, in the center of Herkimer County, N. Y., about six miles north of the Little Falls settlement.

Jonathan Burrell, who was a dairy farmer, was possibly more of a specialist than was customary in those early days. At any rate, while his son Harry was still quite a young man, they became interested together in the manufacture of cheese. Other farmers took this up and soon the cheese industry became quite important in that section. Harry Burrell was still a young man when he was sent to New York by the farmers to sell the season's make of cheese. The cheese was hauled on wagons or sleighs to Albany or Troy, and loaded on scows for New York.

Harry Burrell remained in partnership with his father in the cheese business, until about 1833, when he took the business over entirely, and handled in New York City other dairy products as well as cheese. It is interesting to note that Harry Burrell, with his two older sons, was the first exporter of cheese to England, and that a large business was developed with that country.

In 1868, D. H. Burrell, who had been in business with his father since 1860, went to Europe, where he made the most of his opportunity to

3

Mike''s 1st milking machine manual   Burrell acquired 7-1999

Found 1979

Let's take a look at the finding of the Burrell B-L-K in my collection. My first knowledge of the "Burrell" milking machine was in about 1978 or 1979. My wife, children and I were on vacation out near Canandaigua, NY and we stopped at an antique tractor show and flea market. While browsing the paper goods dealer's collection I found the above manual for the Burrell B-L-K milking machine. My first purchase of a milking machine manual! About 19 years later my wife (a United Methodist pastor) was visiting an older parishioner. While they were talking about his growing up in that area he mentioned that he still had the original milking machine that he learned to milk cows with. Wouldn't you know it was the Burrell! She came home and told me about it. Well, my heart stopped. It took about six months for me to actually see this elusive machine. I saw it; it was absolutely beautiful and complete. I tried to buy it but was told that they couldn't sell it to me. **But** I could have it for nothing to put in my collection. It is funny how good things happen if you are patient.

Burrell

study the dairy industry in both England and France. He was so impressed with what he learned that, on coming back to New York City, he arranged to return to Little Falls for the purpose of introducing improved methods to the dairymen of central New York. In 1869 he founded the business which later became D. H. Burrell & Co.

The years that followed were years of great progress. It is possible to mention here only the most important things which D. H. Burrell and his associates were instrumental in accomplishing.

In 1870, the importation of supplies for the manufacture of cheese was begun. At about the same time D. H. Burrell started an active campaign to establish cheese factories, for which his firm also began to make and sell supplies and equipment.

In 1876, D. H. Burrell put on the market the famous Seamless Cheese Bandage, and in 1880 the firm introduced Gang Presses and Hoops. These things were of incalculable aid in developing the cheese industry in this country. About 1880 the manufacture of cheese box material was begun and soon reached an output of several million sets yearly.

In 1880, my brother and I, introduced the ensilage system of preserving and feeding corn, and built the first large, practical silos.

In 1881, an arrangement was made with Chr. Hansen's Laboratory of Copenhagen, Denmark, which secured for us the sale for the United States and Canada of Chr. Hansen's Danish Dairy Preparations.

In 1881, we obtained control of and introduced commercially in America the first centrifugal cream separator, which has been followed through successive stages to the present Burrell-Simplex Link-Blade Separator.

D. H. Burrell & Co. have also been largely instrumental in the development of Milk Pasteurizing Systems and are large manufacturers of dairy and creamery as well as cheese factory equipment.

It was in 1860, the year that D. H. Burrell went into business with his father, that he first became interested in a milking machine, and a patented device was tried out at the Burrell farm at Little Falls. That was over sixty years ago; and although the Burrell (B-L-K) Milker was not made and sold until 1905, it is today the oldest power-operated milker that has been continuously on the American market.

David H. Burrell died in 1919. He has left as a monument the practical achievements of a busy life devoted to the upbuilding of dairying. He has set a measure of service which it is our hope and our intention to maintain. With all these years and generations of service behind us, we must go forward to no less worthy, though perhaps less spectacular, achievements.

My association in business with David H. Burrell, my brother, began in 1881. With his sons Loomis and David H., I look with confidence to the carrying on of the founder's purposes and ideals, and to a future of growing usefulness of D. H. Burrell & Co. Inc. to the dairy industry of America.

President

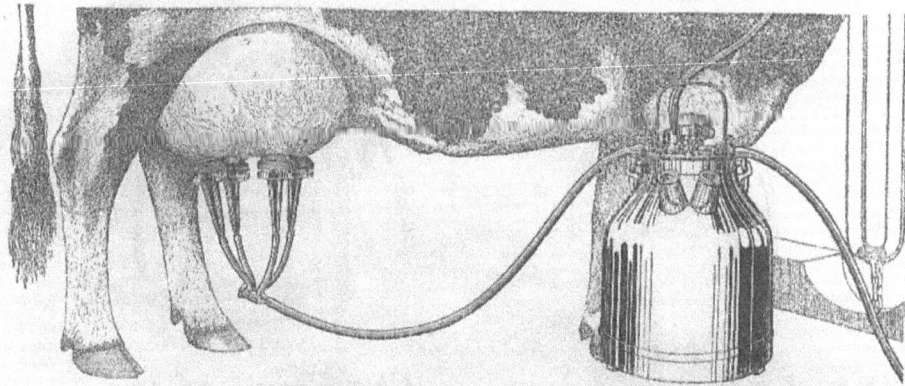

The Need for a Milking Machine

THE OLD saying that "necessity is the mother of invention" was never more true than in the case of the milking machine. To the man, whose chief business is the production of milk, a practical machine milker is not only a necessity but a veritable godsend. Even in small herds, where machine milking costs as much as hand milking, the milking machine is of great advantage and indirectly very profitable.

The bugbear of the dairyman has always been labor. Even when plenty of help was obtainable, it was often indifferent and unreliable. Incompetent and abusive hand-milkers have spoiled many a good cow. The dairyman never knew when he would be left alone with all the milking to do himself. As labor has become more scarce, and consequently more independent, a competent hand-miker has become a jewel beyond price.

There is little need to discuss why this is true. The long hours, the seven-day-a-week grind, and the drudgery of hand-milking have not attracted men from shorter hours and more interesting work in other industries.

But all this is now changed. With the milking machine the dairyman can declare his independence of indifferent labor and attract to his farm a better class of farm help. He can increase his herd to the full capacity of his farm. He can produce a better quality of milk. He can keep his cows' udders and teats in better condition.

He can cut the cost of milk production. He can have more leisure for recreation, for planning and for study. He can make the farm more attractive to his growing boys.

The Burrell Milker is a practical, efficient, economical necessity. It is a perfect substitute for the calf — better than hand-milking. It has long ago passed the experimental stage. It is of simple parts and easy to operate. To the business dairyman, it is the next step in the economical management of his business.

There are three ways to make more money from dairying. One way is to produce milk for less money — with the Burrell Milker, you can reduce your labor costs. Another way is to produce more milk — with the Burrell Milker, you can develop your herd in spite of the shortage of labor. The third way is to produce a better grade of milk — with the Burrell Milker and the Burrell System of Sterilization, you can easily produce milk of certified quality.

The Burrell Milker is here to stay. After seventeen years of success, its advantages and its benefits have been fully demonstrated. Let it serve you as it has already served thousands of others.

A H Barber

Three types of milkers which we have developed and discarded during the evolution of the present Burrell Milker

The Story of the Burrell Milker

EVERY new device or machine must go through a period of improvement and refinement. The original machine, wonderful as it may seem at its inception, becomes crude and awkward when compared with later models. For instance, the first automobiles were but contraptions compared with the modern car.

The Burrell Milker has gone through this period of improvement and refinement. It has long since passed the stage of novelty and become a practical, dependable, every-day necessity. First put on the market in 1905, it has been subjected to years of relentless test by both experience and experiment. Parts which have proved faulty have been ruthlessly discarded — those which have proved efficient have been retained.

Believing that a knowledge of the history of the Burrell Milker is necessary to a full understanding of its present merits, we give you briefly the story of our work to develop an efficient and simple milking machine.

Our interest in a milker was first aroused by a machine patented in 1860 by L. O. Colvin and tested by D. H. Burrell on his father's farm. This machine consisted of teat-cups, connected directly to a hand suction-pump, which could be mounted either on a pail or held in such a way that the milk was discharged freely into the pail beneath. Although this machine was not a success, it served to crystalize our interest in the development of a practical milking machine. Since 1860, we have tested in actual use all of the more promising milker inventions.

7

The story of continues

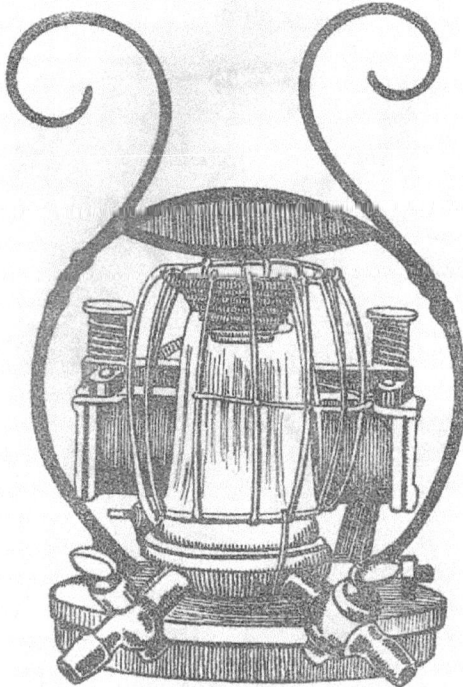

*The original Lawrence & Kennedy pulsator
discarded by us in 1904*

Among the early devices were various kinds of milking tubes which were inserted into the milk duct of the teat. With some, the milk was expected to run out by gravity, while with others, suction was applied. All of these were found to be very dangerous because they were sources of infection and caused inflammation of the udder. These so-called milking machines gained a bad reputation, because many cows were ruined by their use.

Also, there were many machines invented for squeezing the milk out of the teats. Rollers or pads were used to press the teat, beginning at the top and following downward somewhat in imitation of hand milking. These, however, proved failures for several reasons, among them may be mentioned the difficulty of adjusting the machine to the cow and holding it in proper position. Not only is the cow apt to step around during milking, but the udder does not have the same shape after most of the milk has been drawn that it had to start with, and this requires the re-setting of the teat squeezers; so that, in

general, the labor required to adjust the squeezing machines and keep them in adjustment and care for them was at least as great as to milk by hand.

It may be said here that the calf draws milk by suction — not by manipulation or squeezing; also that this suction is relieved at frequent intervals, when the calf stops to draw its breath. Thus we see that the natural method of drawing milk from the teat is by intermittent suction.

In 1895 a great improvement was made over all prior devices, by the invention of Dr. Alexander Shields, who for the first time admitted air to relieve the vacuum and produce pulsations in the teat-cups. With this milker, known as the "Thistle" milking machine, an extended and thorough test was begun in 1895 in D. H. Burrell's dairy of 80 milking cows. While the results obtained with the "Thistle" milker were decidedly better than had been obtained with continuous-suction milkers, they were by no means satisfactory. The relief from suction on the cows' teats was imperfect, since the pulsations were produced in the entire piping system and were never sharp or well-defined.

Next, William Lawrence and Robert Kennedy of Glasgow, Scotland, made an invention which was truly revolutionary. A pneumatically operated pulsator was placed on the cover of the milk pail. By locating the pulsator near the cow,

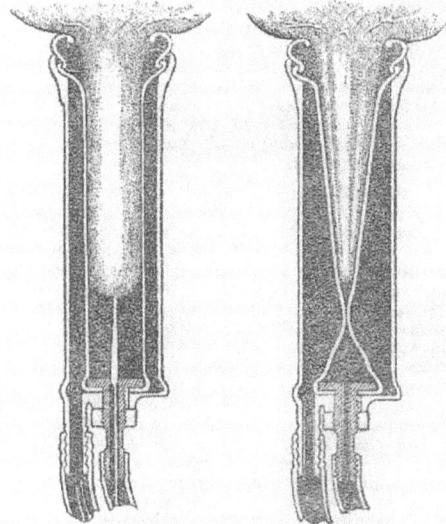

*Double-tube teat cups with rubber lining
discarded by us in 1909*

The story of continues

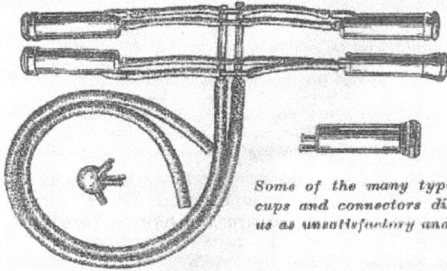

Some of the many types of teat-cups and connectors discarded by us as unsatisfactory and inefficient

the vacuum pulsations, instead of taking place through the entire piping system, occurred only in the short tubing to the teat cups. These pulsations were well-defined. In 1902 we conducted thorough tests with this machine at our Overlook Farm and kept daily records of all cows milked. Although we were not satisfied with the results and offered none of these machines for sale, this was the beginning of the Burrell-Lawrence-Kennedy (B-L-K) Milker.

Note that the result of the invention of Lawrence and Kennedy was to place the pulsator near the udder, where the suction and relief would act quickly in the teat-cups; also, and very important, the pulsator was operated by the suction itself.

Many changes suggested themselves in these first machines, and innumerable trials and experiments were made. Our milking machine department was now thoroughly organized with the best of skill, equipment and materials at its command. The years immediately following the Lawrence and Kennedy invention brought forth many improvements of the utmost importance, although the principle of the original machine remained the same.

We thought that possibly it would be simpler to have a pump for each milker and let the pump-piston produce the pulsating action in the teat-cups. We tested such devices but they were unsatisfactory. After long trials we found that best results could be obtained by never permitting the vacuum to go above a fixed point, which we ultimately proved to be fifteen inches. The simplest way to insure this was to have *one* power-driven pump, a vacuum reservoir near the pump, a pipe-line through the stable, and an automatic relief or safety valve — these became permanent features of the Burrell system. We found that, with a pump for each individual unit, the milk spray was drawn with the air into the pump cylinder and then passed back into the milk as it was discharged into the pail — this was unsanitary. For these reasons we discarded the individual pumps.

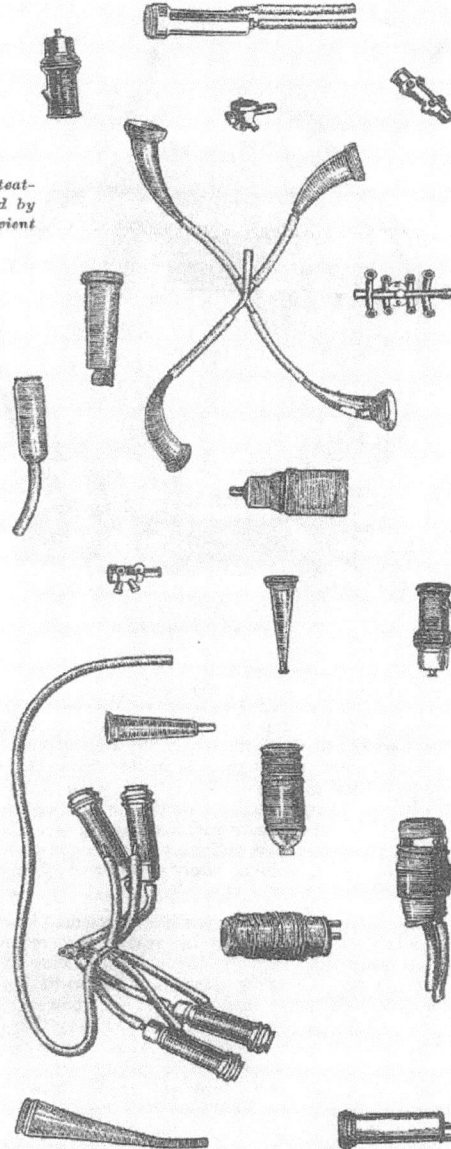

25

Burrell B-L-K
From 1918 Burrell reference booklet in Mike Gleason collection

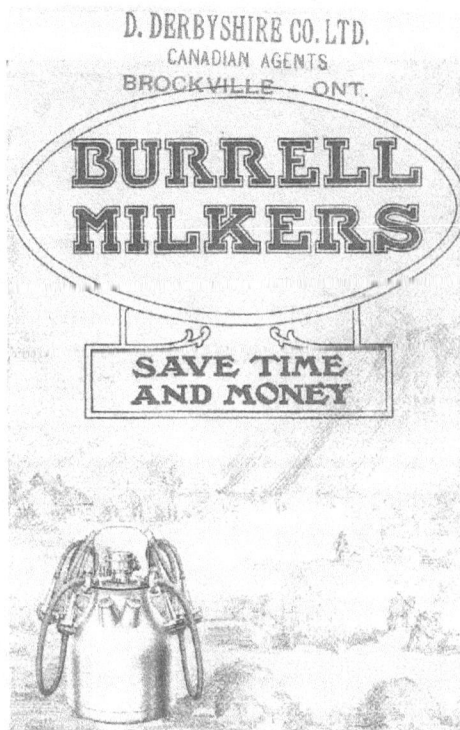

D. DERBYSHIRE CO. LTD.
CANADIAN AGENTS
BROCKVILLE - ONT.

BURRELL MILKERS

SAVE TIME AND MONEY

The Old and the New

The cut at the right is from a photograph taken in 1905 of our rubber lined teat cup machine.

This type of milker was discarded by D. H. Burrell & Co. later in the year 1905. It was way back when very few inventors were thinking of milking machines that D. H. Burrell & Co. decided and proved

that the rubber lined teat cups were not satisfactory.

The present Burrell system is the result of these many years of expensive and painstaking research.

The cut at the left is from a photograph of our latest type machine.

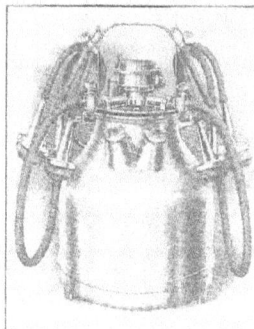

Complete outfit

Milker Patents

WE own a large number of broad patents, granted by the United States and Canada, covering Milking Machines, Vacuum Pumps, etc.

The claims cover inventions by Alexander Shiels and Lawrence & Kennedy, of Scotland; Carl B. Stroyberg, of Denmark: Alexander Gillies of Australia; F. O. A. Weber, Loomis Burrell, F. A. Lane, Daniel Klein, Harvey Feldmeier and Charles B. Dalzell of this country.

All persons are warned against the manufacture, sale or use of machines or devices infringing the claims of these patents.

D. H. BURRELL & CO., Inc.

Burton-Page Milker
Established 1914
Chicago, ILL.

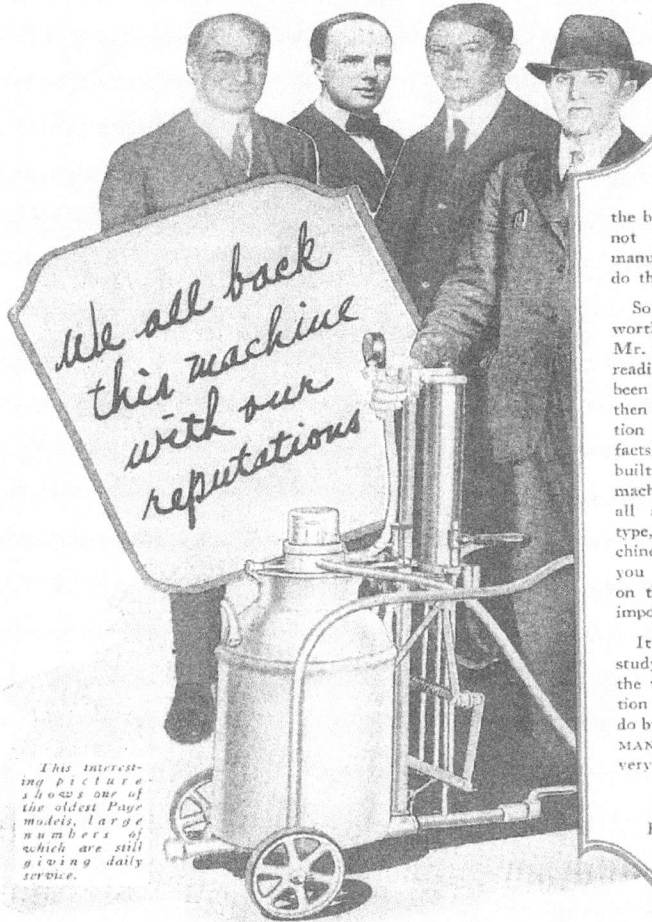

This interesting picture shows one of the oldest Page models, large numbers of which are still giving daily service.

we all back this machine with our reputations

Foreword:

Mr. Dairyman:

We know cows; we know milkers.

Maybe we do not know just how to put things in the best words to convince you. We're not talkers. We're dairymen and manufacturers; and we let our machines do the talking.

So if you want to get your money's worth out of this booklet, it's up to you, Mr. Dairyman, to help us out a bit by reading real carefully. If we have not been able to explain in best language, then favor us by going over the description a second time. For we have the facts, sound facts; we have a machine built *not* on "bunk"-selling talk; but a machine built on truly different, basical all around improvements. A newer-type, better, *simpler*, easier milking machine—a milking machine that brings you all the advantages of any milker on the market and several distinct and important advantages of its own.

It's important to you—therefore—to study out the points about the spring, the valveless milk chamber, no installation expense and so on. Then if you do buy a milker you will be many, many, MANY dollars ahead, while getting the very best of all milkers.

Sincerely yours,

BURTON-PAGE COMPANY

(Established 1914)

CHICAGO, ILL.

J. W. ESKHOLME
English engineer, who designed and perfected the electric model.

ALBERT BLATZ, Jr.
President and General Manager in charge of factory.

B. E. PAGE
First President

W. A. SHIPPERT
Expert dairyman, inventor of the valveless milk chamber.

A Romance of Business is told fully and frankly on the following pages.

Burton-Page Milker
Established 1914
Chicago, ILL.

What Happens in the Udder

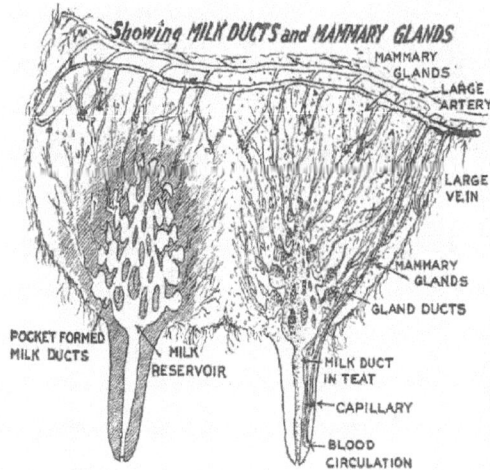

Showing MILK DUCTS and MAMMARY GLANDS

MAMMARY GLANDS
LARGE ARTERY
LARGE VEIN
MAMMARY GLANDS
GLAND DUCTS
POCKET FORMED MILK DUCTS
MILK RESERVOIR
MILK DUCT IN TEAT
CAPILLARY
BLOOD CIRCULATION

PAGE TWELVE

When a cow is being milked, three processes must function harmoniously.

First, Secretion. This occurs within the mammary glands and cannot be controlled by the cow or the milker. However, this secretion of milk is closely connected with the cow's nervous system. If she is frightened or made uneasy, the secretion does not proceed normally.

Second, Release. After the milk is secreted in the mammary glands, it is stored in a system of branching and rebranching milk tubes and is conducted by them to the milk reservoir just above the teats. At the point where these tubes enter the reservoir, there are ring muscles which the cow may open or close at will. If the cow is discomforted in any way she is likely, by closing these muscles, to hold up her milk, or to give down slowly.

Third, Extraction. Apart from the small amount of milk (about one pint) stored in the reservoir, the milk cannot be extracted without the aid and willingness of the cow.

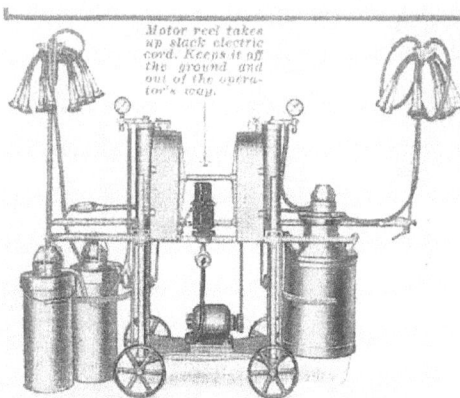

Motor reel takes up slack electric cord. Keeps it off the ground and out of the operator's way.

Here is a 4-cow Electric Milker, showing the equipment used when milking each cow into a separate container. Either two or four-cow models can be equipped this way.

PAGE TWENTY-EIGHT

Individual Milker

For the man who wants to weigh and test the milk of each cow separately after each milking the necessary added parts can be furnished at nominal cost. Such a record is required when an accurate check is being kept of each cow's production. Our device for this arrangement is simple and inexpensive. It is supplied on special order when the machine is shipped or can be put on later. It fits any model—two or four cow. Many large dairymen keep an extremely accurate and complete day-to-day record on every cow in order to locate and eliminate the "boarders" and bring their herds to highest efficiency. The Page Individual Cow Milker enables you to accomplish that at a minimum expense.

From reference manual collection of Mike Gleason

B-V Milking Machine Company

Milwaukee, WI.

One reference is made in *Hoard's Dairyman*, November 14, 1919. Nothing else is known.

The Farm Woman's Friend

The B-V Milker

Save Time — Health — Money

The B-V Milking Machine

Milking is the most tedious part of the night and morning chores. The B-V Milker converts it into a quickly and efficiently done job. One man operating three units can milk twenty-five cows in a single hour.

On many farms women do the milking, a fatiguing and irksome task when done by hand. Their health is often impaired. B-V Milker will do the work, save health and hands and get better results.

With a B-V Milker the owner can get along with less hired help and reduce the cost of milking to a minimum. The cost of operating the machine is almost negligible.

The B-V Milking Machine is made of a non-corrosive, rust-proof metal. It retains its original brightness and smooth finish. There is no need for nickel-plate, which makes this the most sanitary and desirable metal for milking machines.

You can use a B-V Milker in your dairy. Write us for information and estimates. We guarantee our machine to do the work.

THE B-V MILKING MACHINE CO.
Milwaukee, Wisconsin

RAY WHITTERN · · 6238 Cottage Grove Avenue, Chicago, Illinois
Wholesale Distributor for Illinois, Indiana, Michigan and Ohio

ad from *Hoard's Dairyman*, November 14, 1919.

C

Calf-Way Milker Company

168 North Michigan Boulevard, Chicago, IL.

A CORNER OF THE CALF-WAY MILKER BOOTH AT THE PANAMA-PACIFIC INTERNATIONAL EXPOSITION, SAN FRANCISCO, SHOWING GRAND PRIZE BANNER

The Calf-Way Milker in use on Farm of T. S. Getzelman of Illinois, Milking one of His 30-pound Holstein Cows

Note the reference to the 30 lb cow in the Getzelman herd. How times have changed. Thirty pounds per milking just wouldn't cut it in today's world.

Chore Boy

The Dairy Equipment Company, 3105 Hosmer, Lansing, MI, made the Chore Boy Portable Milker. Chore Boy had a unique set-up with a three-wheel cart that had a platform for a gas engine.

Choreboy

This unit is about 1950 from Mike Gleason collection, I have no other reference materials on this machine.

Photo 1, Paul Dettloff Collection, Arcadia, Wisconsin.

Photo 1 shows an early model with solid cast iron wheels. Red plastic teat cups were used and a 10 gallon milk can was the receiving jar. Two vacuum cylinders sat on top of a blue body.

Photo 2, Paul Dettloff Collection, Arcadia, Wisconsin.

The milker in Photo 2 has basically the same body as in Photo 1, only the cast wheels are missing. A Briggs & Stratton Model "N" gas engine was attached when purchased.

Colvin Hydrauic Milking Machine Patented 1866
invented by Colvin who was inventor of the American Milker

[NEW SERIES.]

Hydraulic Cow Milking Machine.

Every dairyman knows the trouble and labor of milking a dairy of cows by hand, and the difficulty of procuring good milkers, who will always milk the cows alike, clean, quickly, and thoroughly, with comfort to the animal. They have experienced the aching of hands and been troubled with kicking cows. There is no labor done on the farm more uninviting and monotonous; yet it cannot be delayed or put off to a "more convenient season." While machinery has been adapted to the manufacture of butter and cheese, the labor of milking has heretofore been left to muscular exertion alone, the Hydraulic Cow Milker, however, which is illustrated in the engraving is intended to relieve the farmer from the irksome work of hand milking.

American Scientific
May 2, 1868

COLVIN'S PATENT HYDRAULIC COW MILKER.

The accompanying engraving is an illustration of three machines operated with power and attended by one man; two machines, each milking a cow, and one turned back out of the way, for the cow that has been milked to pass out to make way for another to come into the stall to be milked, not stopping the power while changing the cows. The stanchion is the same as any ordinary stanchion, with the exception that it opens out to let the cow pass through to facilitate the changing of cows. In this manner cows can be very quickly brought to the machine, — occupying less time than it would to go to the cow in the yard or stable.

The cows soon learn to come to the machine if fed or salted a few times while being milked. The milk runs into large cans partially sunk in the floor. Three machines are sufficient to milk sixty cows in the time it would take six men to milk them by hand, and one man can attend to all the machines, which may be run by hand, dog, or other power.

The milkers are worked by pumps, the pistons of which are driven by power. They are attached by a jointed iron pipe to allow of the movement of the cow forward, backward, or sideways, always adapting itself to her motions. The teat cups are of corrugated rubber closely enveloping the teats, and will fit those of any cow. The pumps oscillate, giving the natural motion of the calf in sucking or of the hand in milking; the space between the elastic diaphragm in the milker and the pump being filled with water, which in working the pumps, oscillates in the tube and produces a vacuum at each alternate stroke of the piston. No dust, hairs, or dirt can possibly find their way into the milk while passing to the receiving cans. The machine has been exhibited in this city and attracted considerable attention. Having witnessed its practical operation, we are willing to add our testimonial to that of others in regard to the facility of working and the apparent value of the machine. Its operation appears to be as agreeable to the cow as it is effective in saving time and labor.

Patented May 22, 1866, and Feb. 18, 1868; patents for minor improvements now pending through the Scientific American Patent Agency. All orders or communications for information should be addressed to the Hydraulic Cow Milker Manufacturing Co., No. 1 Vesey st., Astor House block, New York city.

Colvin hydraulic Milker
1865

COLVIN'S PATENT HYDRAULIC COW MILKER.

| other privation, and defy the fury of the raging elements— | considerable portion of this oil and oi

CONDÉ

"THE WORLD'S FINEST MILKING EQUIPMENT"

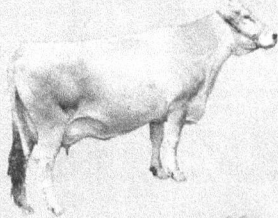

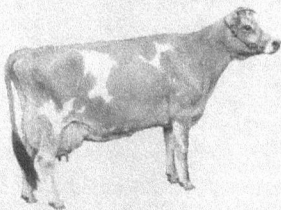

Condé

Modern Conde factory at Sherrill, N.Y.

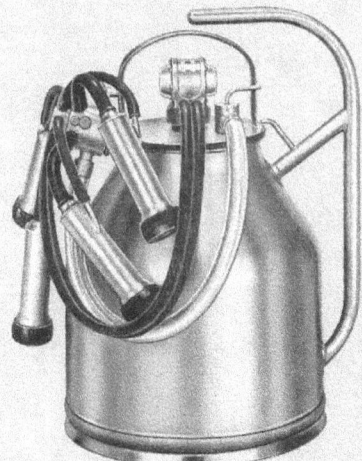

Floor type milking unit with patented rigid handle pail.

Conde
Made in Sherrill, NY
in 1938
also sold in Canada as "Cockshutt Conde Milker"

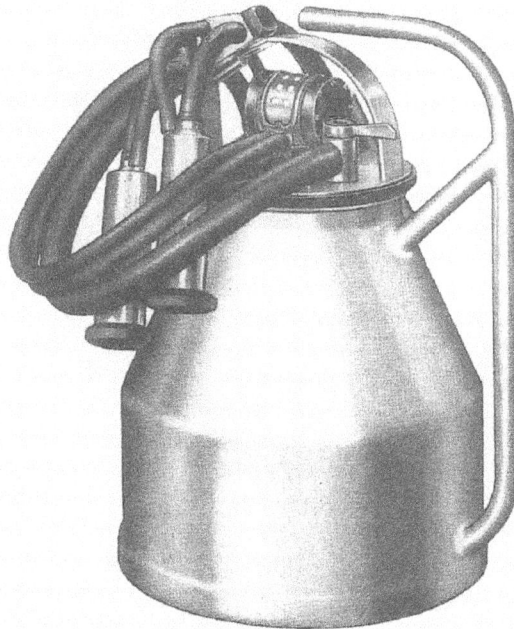

The modern design of the CONDÉ Single Unit, with its many exclusive features acclaimed by thousands of dairymen throughout the United States and Canada, is a decided asset in the hands of any good dairyman. Never have you used a milker so convenient. The pail is broad on the bottom to prevent tipping. The rigid handle extends to the topmost part of the unit where it is handy to grasp with or without the cover, and because of this new type of handle the pail can be easily emptied with one hand. The teat cup assembly is always right side up and ready to apply; simply unhook it from the handle and open the milk spigot. The filtered air feature of the CONDÉ Pulsator keeps the mechanism free from dust and dirt, giving the moving parts a long life. The cover is equipped with the exclusive CONDÉ condensing unit, which keeps the milk vapor in the pail, leaving the pipe line dry. Milk may be observed, as it travels from the cow to the pail, through the sanitary observation disc in the top of the milk spigot. All of these features add up to the very last word in sanitation and convenience.

From an early "Conde Milker" colored advertizing flyer in my collection

Conde
Made in Sherrill, NY in 1938
also sold in Canada as "Cockshutt Conde Milker"

Conde 1938 galvanized

Conde Milker in Mike Gleason Milker Collection

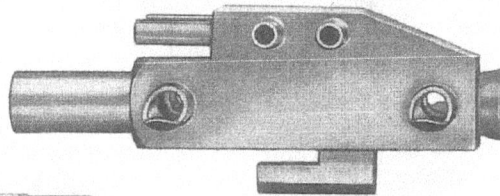

The Milk Claw (right) is very expensive to build, but it is worth the cost. All milk passages are straight through. All openings are large and easily cleaned. The end is closed air tight with a sanitary rubber cap.

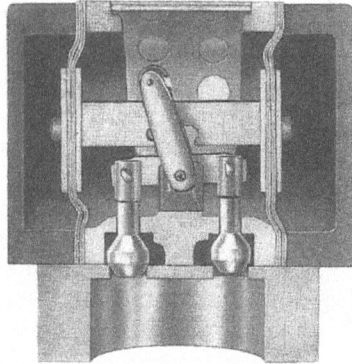

This cutaway view (left) of the CONDÉ patented Pulsator enables you to clearly see the absolute simplicity of its construction. Self-closing solid poppet-type valves that need no adjustment, double diaphragms that are not affected by heat or cold, a removable filter that eliminates hair, dust and dirt, and accurate single-screw speed adjustment, are all features that assure positive operation and uninterrupted service.

CONDÉ Inflations are produced from high quality fat-resisting rubber by the largest and best equipped companies in the United States. The No. 13 Inflation is soft, gathering around the cow's teat to feel like a kid glove feels to the human finger. The No. 10 Inflation has a slightly thicker side wall and a flat squeeze. The No. 13 Inflation is recommended in most cases and all machines are factory equipped with this type. There are some herds that milk better with a No. 10 Inflation. CONDÉ dealers and distributors are well qualified to choose the proper inflation for your dairy. Both types of inflations are designed with ribs at the bottom so that the natural stretch of the rubber can be taken up at various intervals during their life.

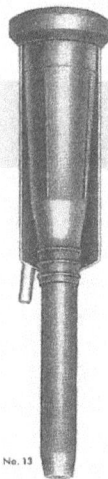

No. 13

No. 10

From an early "Conde Milker" colored advertizing flyer in my collection

Conde
Made in Sherrill, NY
in 1938
also sold in Canada as "Cockshutt Conde Milker"

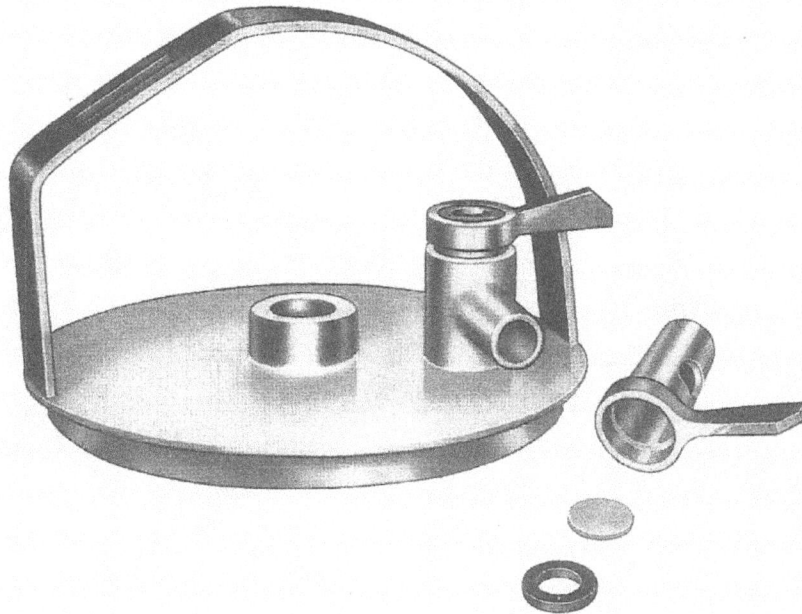

The CONDÉ Cover comprises five parts all welded together into one piece. Surfaces are smooth, no screw heads or other crevices to catch dirt. The bottom flange on the cover is drawn in at a 15° angle to match the angle on the pail cover gasket, holding the gasket in place without grooves or recessed flanges. The slot provided on the cover handle holds the teat cup assembly. The milk spigot is in three pieces, two of which are an observation disc and retainer. The top of the spigot where these parts fit is recessed at an angle which holds the observation disc and retainer in place, making it self-sealing. When the spigot handle is parallel with the milk tube, it is open and when closed, the handle on the milk spigot will be against the pail cover handle as shown in the photograph.

From an early "Conde Milker" colored advertizing flyer in my collection

Conde
Made in Sherrill, NY
in 1938
also sold in Canada as "Cockshutt Conde Milker"

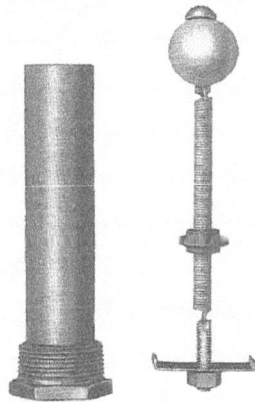

The Pail Cover Gasket, Pulsator Gasket, Claw End Cap and Condenser Cup are shown below. The Pail Cover Gasket is thick and wide, molded at an angle on the inside to match the angle on the lower flange of the pail cover. The Pulsator Gasket is placed over the boss on the pail cover and the pulsator rests on it at that point, creating an air-tight seal. The Claw End Cap is a modern CONDÉ idea, doing away with threads and other hard to clean parts. The Condenser Cup, a patented CONDÉ part, fits inside the boss on top of the cover and is one of the most exclusive features of the CONDÉ Milker, keeping the milk vapor in the pail where it belongs, leaving the pipe line dry. It also acts as a check valve.

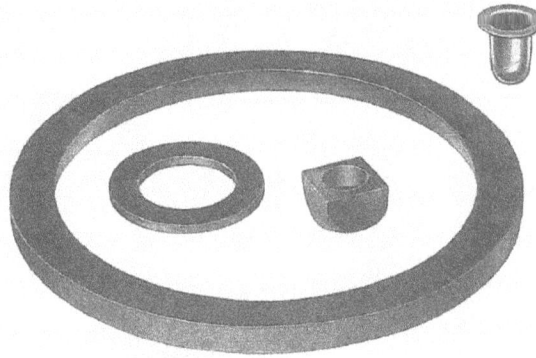

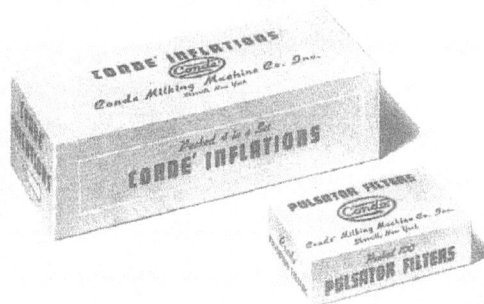

The CONDÉ Relief Valve controls the vacuum in the tank and line, and may be adjusted by turning the nut on the extreme bottom to the right to increase the vacuum and to the left to decrease it. This Relief Valve is located in the bottom of the tank, is simple in construction and very accurate.

CONDÉ Inflations, either No. 10 or No. 13, may be purchased in sets of four, boxed as illustrated. Every CONDÉ owner should have one or more boxes of inflations and Pulsator Filters on hand. The Filters, packaged in boxes of 100, are made of special material, designed to allow only good clean air in the Pulsator to insure proper operation.

From an early "Conde Milker" colored advertizing flyer in my collection

Conde
Made in Sherrill, NY
in 1938
also sold in Canada as "Cockshutt Conde Milker"

This modern CONDÉ Vacuum Supplier, powered with either an electric motor or gasoline motor, is complete in every detail and ready to install.

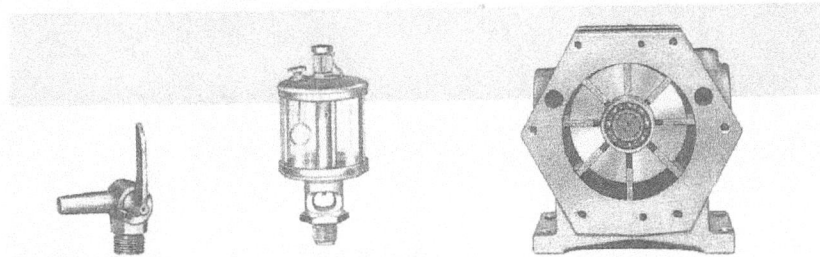

The CONDÉ Stall Cock turns to a positive stop in both open and closed positions, making it fast and convenient for the operator.

The CONDÉ Oiler is automatic in its operation and supplies the pump with adequate lubrication at all times.

Efficiency and simplicity are the two words that best describe the CONDÉ Vacuum Pump. The rotating part of this pump revolves on heavy ball bearings constantly lubricated with fresh clean oil. Tough composition vanes, thrown away from the center by centrifugal force, create the vacuum. Air movement is evenly distributed to effect the best possible cooling.

From an early "Conde Milker" colored advertizing flyer in my collection

Conde
Made in Sherrill, NY
in 1938
also sold in Canada as "Cockshutt Conde Milker"

Cockshutt Company

Cockshutt Company of Canada marketed the Condé
System from Sherrill, NY.

REPAIR PARTS

for

Cockshutt Condé Milker

COCKSHUTT
PLOW COMPANY LIMITED
TRURO · MONTREAL   BRANTFORD WINNIPEG · REGINA · SASKATOON
SMITHS FALLS   CANADA   CALGARY · EDMONTON

From Paul Detloff book "Milking Machine
Guide" published 1998

Conde
Made in Sherrill, NY
in 1938
also sold in Canada as "Cockshutt Conde Milker"

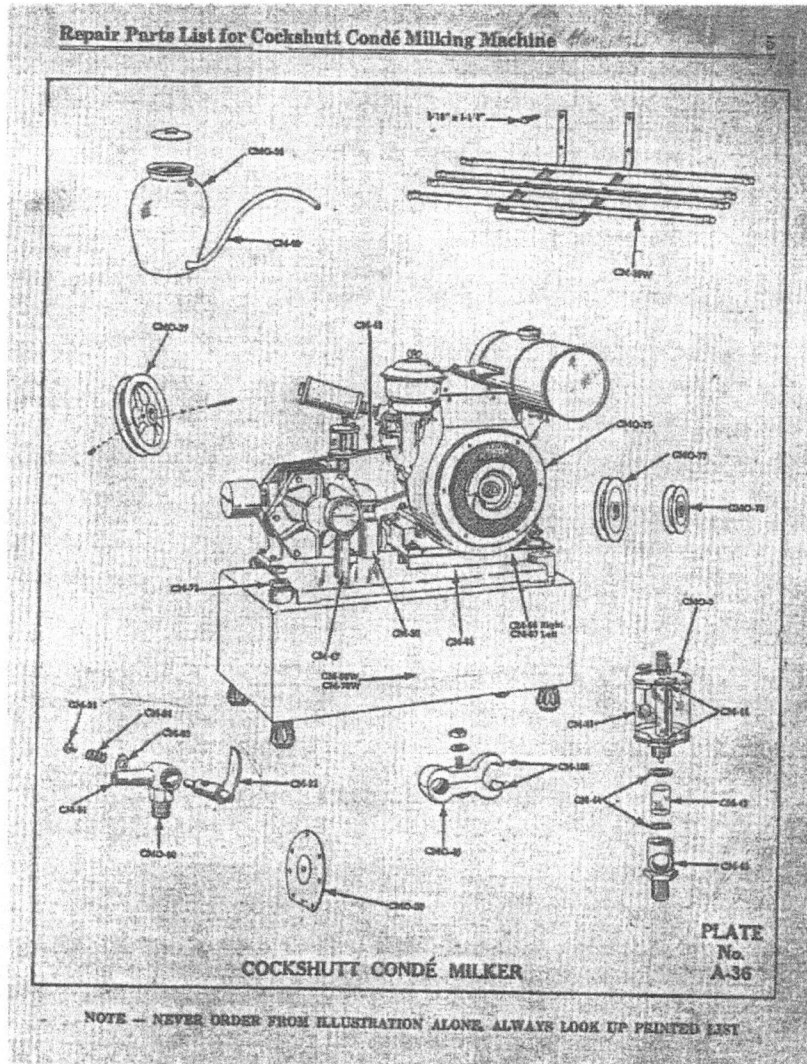

Repair Parts List for Cockshutt Condé Milking Machine

COCKSHUTT CONDÉ MILKER

PLATE No. A-36

NOTE — NEVER ORDER FROM ILLUSTRATION ALONE, ALWAYS LOOK UP PRINTED LIST

From Paul Detloff book "Milking Machine
Guide" published 1998

Conde
Made in Sherrill, NY
in 1938
also sold in Canada as "Cockshutt Conde Milker"

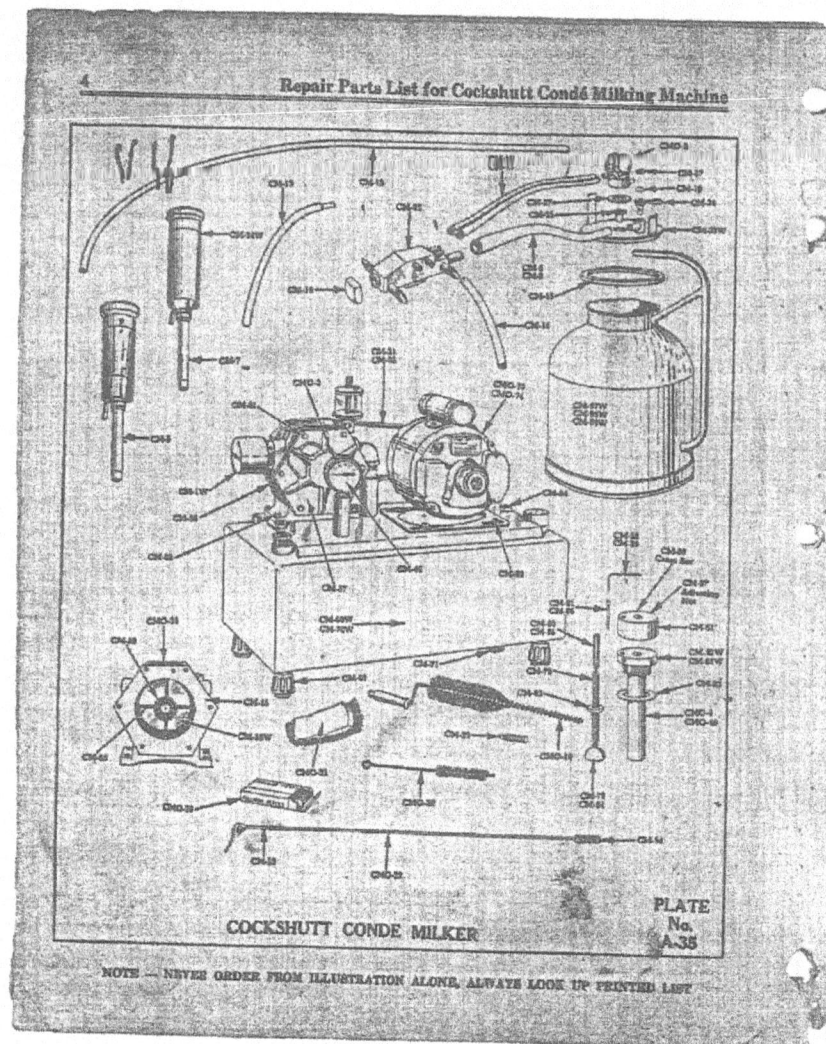

Repair Parts List for Cockshutt Condé Milking Machine

COCKSHUTT CONDE MILKER

PLATE No. A-35

NOTE — NEVER ORDER FROM ILLUSTRATION ALONE, ALWAYS LOOK UP PRINTED LIST

From Paul Detloff book "Milking Machine
Guide" published 1998

D

Dairy Equipment Company
See Chore Boy.

Dairy Maid Milker Company
Station F, Toledo, OH

They were quite proud of their transparent "Marios" Cups.

With a
Dairy Maid Milker
using "Marios" Transparent Cups, You Can
See Each Teat Milking

Only milker with visible milking for each teat, and an extension cup top which massages the udder. Drive-rod type, valve simpler, more sanitary than others. Milks faster and cleaner. Sold on trial. Send for free catalog, sample cup, guarantee, prices, etc. (Give layout of barn and specify number of cows).

Dairy Maid Milker Co., Station "F", Toledo, O.

NOTICE: To Hinman, B-L-K and other vacuum type users. We will supply sets of "Marios" transparent cups complete ready to connect to your milker at $10 a set. Cleaner, faster, more sanitary milking guaranteed. Sold on 5 days trial.

ad from *Hoard's Dairyman*, June 8, 1918.

Dairy Queen Milking Machine Company
Made the Dairy Queen Milker. Nothing else is known.

Decker Manufacturing Company
Janesville, WI

Made the Grade A Milker. Nothing else is known.

Some of the graphics in this book were copied from Dr. Paul Dettloff's book "Milking Machine Guide"

De Laval Milkers

"THE BETTER WAY OF MILKING"

WE USE THE
DE LAVAL
MILKER

WE U
DE L
Cream

DE LAVAL MILKERS

*De Laval first gave us
the better way of separating
cream from milk, and now
the better way of milking*

THE
DE LAVAL SEPARATOR COMPANY

*165 BROADWAY, NEW YORK
600 JACKSON BLVD., CHICAGO
61 BEALE STREET, SAN FRANCISCO*

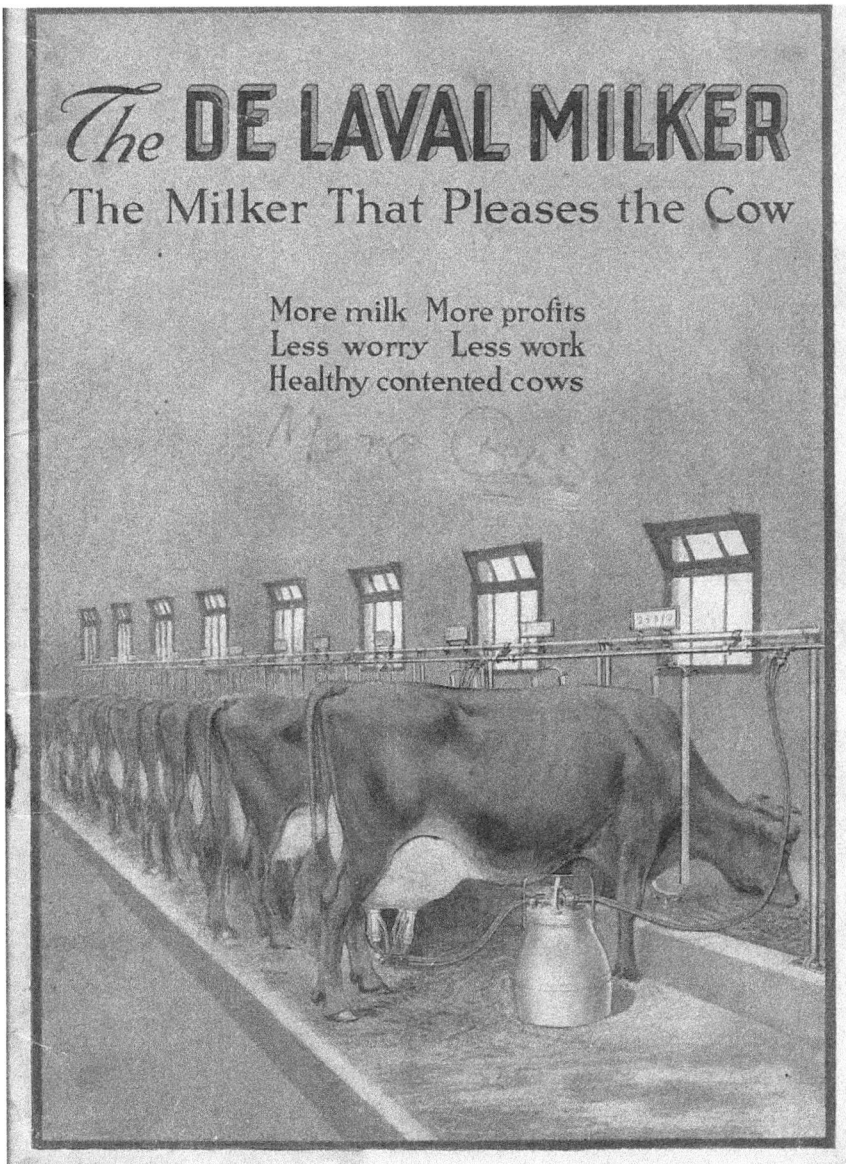

DeLaval

THE DE LAVAL MILKER

Eliminates the drudgery of milking, does the work in one-third the time and keeps the boys on the farm

DESIGNED, manufactured and sold by the oldest, largest and best-known makers of dairy machinery in the world.

For further information and estimates, address nearest office.

The De Laval Separator Co.
165 Broadway, New York
29 E. Madison St., Chicago

De Laval Pacific Co.
61 Beale St., San Francisco

The De Laval Co., Ltd.
Canada
Montreal   Peterboro
Winnipeg   Edmonton
        Vancouver

Complete Installation of De Laval Milker

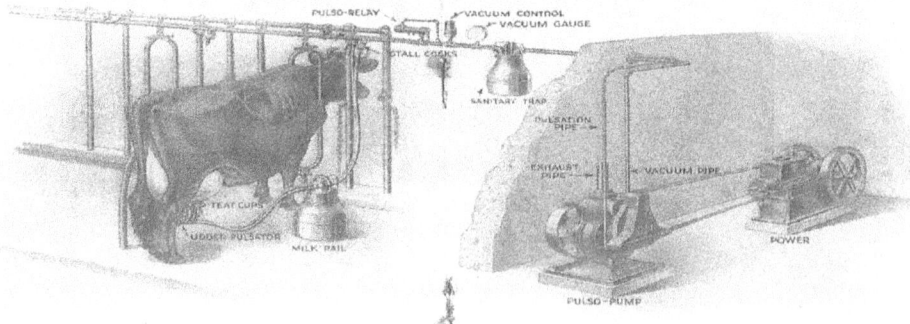

THE simplicity of installation and operation of the De Laval Milker is more apparent from a view of the entire installation than from detailed consideration of the various parts. The independent pipe-line controlling the action of the pulsator is clearly shown in the illustration. The milk is drawn alternately from the front and rear teats, and passes into the pail. The vacuum is controlled by the vacuum control, any variations being plainly shown by the gauge.

The sanitary trap collects any moisture that may be in the line—preventing any foreign substance from entering the vacuum chamber of the Pulso-Pump. The pulsation pipe-line connects the Udder Pulsator with the Pulso-Relay and the pulsating mechanism of the Pulso-Pump. This pipe-line is entirely independent of the continuous vacuum pipe-line. The simplicity of installation and operation of the De Laval Milker is of importance in both large and small dairies.

DeLaval

Before the first De Laval Milker was sold 24 years were spent by the De Laval organization in continuous research and experiment to perfect a practical, fool-proof De Laval Milker.

SUCTION PRINCIPLE WITH INTERMITTENT PULSATIONS

From 1898 to 1910 De Laval developed and experimented with four different types of milkers, all embodying the principle of suction and    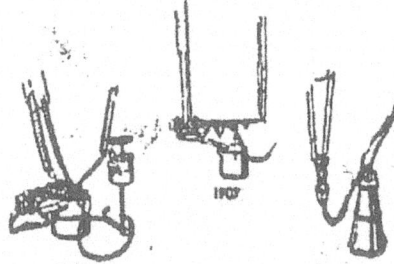 intermittent pulsations. These machines milked but they required adjustment and left too much to the judgment of the operator.

1894

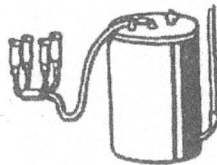

1898

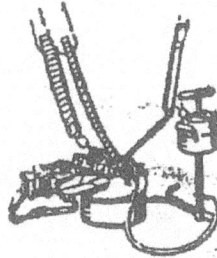

1903

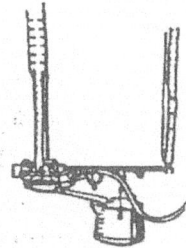

1907

1910

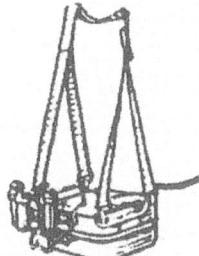

1912

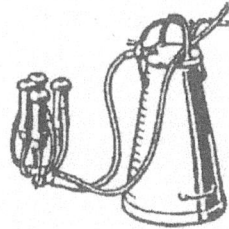

1914

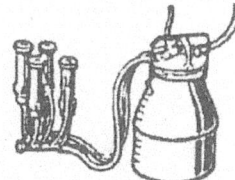

1918

24 YEARS OF RESEARCH

DeLaval

How a Cow Makes Milk

The idea that a cow's production of milk can be materially increased or decreased simply through the act of milking is new to a great many people; yet those who are familiar with cows have long known this to be a fact. All practical dairymen know that some people are better milkers than others and can get more milk from the same cows. They know, too, that once a cow becomes accustomed to a certain milker, invariably her production will be decreased, for a short time at least, if milkers are changed. For this reason dairymen insist that the same cows be milked by the same milkers.

Contrary to popular belief, a cow's udder at milking time is not full of liquid milk, containing only about one-half pint of milk in each of the four reservoirs which are directly connected to the teats. The cow's udder is full of a mass of glands much like a sponge, and of tissue and a net-work of veins, arteries and nerves. It is true that a cow's udder becomes distended at milking time, but this is due to the fact that the cow is constantly converting the feed which she consumes throughout the day and depositing it in milk-forming materials in the milk-secreting glands or alveoli, as they are known. Naturally the more of this material that is stored, the more distended the udder becomes.

As the cow consumes feed during the day, this in turn is made into blood which circulates through her body, and during the course of a day approximately 5000 quarts of blood circulate through the cow's udder, where the milk-forming materials are deposited.

When a cow is ready for milking, as has been shown in the foregoing, her udder is distended and is full of milk-forming materials. There is, however, only a very small quantity of milk in her udder. Practically 85 per cent of the milk she produces is made or manufactured during the milking process. When milking is commenced, the nerves in the teats, which are highly sensitive, flash "messages" (these messages are, of course, simply nerve impulses and are given out unconsciously on the part of the cow) to the cow's milk-secreting organism to "make milk." If the sensation in the teats is pleasing and agreeable, then the message is given out to "produce more milk," and as long as these pleasing sensations or stimuli continue, then the manufacture of milk is continued to the extent of the cow's ability. Should the sen-

sations, however, become disagreeable or painful, then the nerves in the teats send out a message to "stop making milk," and the cow holds up her milk—a process which is well known.

Of course other stimuli aside from those applied to the teats can cause a cow to hold up her milk, such as fear, fright, abuse, strange objects, loud and unusual noises. All of these can cause a cow's nervous system to react and her milk-secreting organism to shrink up, and the passage or duct from the many little glands or alveoli to the reservoir is contracted so that the milk does not flow into the milk cistern.

It has been found by long experience that it is necessary to please the cow in order to get the most milk, and it has also been found that certain stimuli or methods of milking are most pleasing. A cow likes regularity, and it has been determined that approximately 45 to 48 squeezes or pulsations a minute, maintained with unvarying regularity, are most conducive to good milking. It has been found also that the action must be vigorous and yet gentle and soothing. It is well known that a fast milker, other things being equal, will get more milk from a cow than a slow or dribbling one, and this is due to the fact that the cow's milk-secreting system always tries to supply the demand placed upon it. In other words, if the demand for milk on her milk-secreting system is great, she tries to supply this demand to the best of her ability. It is well known that a cow produces a great deal of milk when a calf is young and has not learned to eat other foods, but as the calf grows older and eats other foods its need for milk becomes less, and the cow gradually produces less and finally dries up altogether. If this same cow were milked out clean at every milking, she would produce a great deal more milk and milk for a longer period. Every cow man knows this to be true.

With these facts in mind, then, the De Laval Milker was designed and perfected to milk the cow in the best possible manner, and to do this uniformly, without variation, from milking to milking, from day to day, or from year to year. It is due to this careful research and the fact that the De Laval Milker is designed to work in harmony with a living animal of highly developed nervous temperament, and that it is mechanically perfected, that such remarkable results are being obtained from its use.

DeLaval

Points to be Considered in the Selection of a Milking Machine

A milking machine is used twice a day—365 days a year; it can either save or waste a great deal of time; it can be either a help or a detriment to the cows on which it is used. It comes in contact with high-priced milk, and can either maintain or impair its original quality. Three very important things—the owner's time, his cows, and milk—may be benefited by the right milker. Therefore, thought and time devoted to this subject before the final selection is made are most profitably spent. Consider carefully the following points:

1. **Number of Cows Necessary for a Milker.** As a general rule any herd of ten or more cows can profitably be milked with a milking machine. Frequently milkers are profitably used with less than ten cows. See page 9.

2. **Profit to be Expected from Use of a Milker.** On page 9 will be found the very conservative estimate of $20.30 which a De Laval Milker may be expected to make per cow per year. Many De Laval Milkers have made much more than this, and have paid for themselves in less than a year.

3. **The Company Back of It.** This is an extremely important consideration. Is the company financially strong, reliable, and capable of giving you service and providing parts at a future date? Keep in mind that the De Laval Companies are the oldest and largest manufacturers of dairy equipment, famous for their strength, service and fair dealings.

4. **Number in Use.** The number of machines in use is often a good index to the success of a machine. At the beginning of 1925 there were more than 80,000 De Laval Milkers in use. During the past few years the number has doubled each year. This is a remarkable record when it is considered that most of them were sold during the worst financial depression of recent years, when no equipment of any kind was purchased by farmers except that which was absolutely necessary and would pay for itself.

5. **Operation.** Practically all milkers can be made to work with a skilled and patient operator, but such a milker is no solution of the milking problem. The De Laval Milker is so simple in design and construction that any one capable of putting teat-cups on a cow can operate it.

6. **No Adjusting.** With the De Laval Milker the operator is not required to make a single adjustment. The pump is automatically oiled and cannot burn out its bearings. See page 11. The vacuum controller is automatic, requires no attention on the part of the operator, and too much vacuum cannot be applied to the cow. See page 19. The pulsation speed cannot be changed by the operator, which insures absolute uniformity of milking. The pulsator is extremely simple in operation, does not require oiling and seldom requires attention. See page 15.

7. **Effect on Cows.** Many people are reluctant to buy a milking machine for fear of injuring their cows. Regardless of past experience, no one need have any such fear concerning a De Laval. After eight years, and with thousands in use, the De Laval Companies do not know nor have ever heard of a single case of injury to a cow resulting from the use of a De Laval Milker. See pages 5, 15, 17, 19.

8. **Effect on Lactation Period.** Some people think a milking machine is good only when the cows are fresh and during the early part of their lactation period. This is not true of a De Laval. It milks cows perfectly during any time of the lactation period and will usually lengthen the period.

9. **Number of Pipe Lines.** Whether a milking machine has one, two or more pipe lines is of little concern to most people, and is mentioned here merely because this point is sometimes brought up in connection with milking machines. The De Laval has two pipe lines, because they are necessary for simplicity of construction and proper operation.

10. **Single or Double Units.** Much misinformation has been spread on this subject. See page 19 for a complete discussion, where it will be shown why only single units are used with the De Laval Milker, and why they are more economical in the long run.

11. **Uniformity of Milking.** No dairyman would think of constantly changing hand milkers, because it is a well-known fact that cows like to be milked the same way each milking and respond best to uniformity. The De Laval Milker insures absolute uniformity of milking. See pages 11 and 15.

12. **Permanent or Portable Milker.** A permanent milker has the pump and power in a stationary position with the vacuum and pulsation pipes extending above the stanchions, with outlets near each cow so that the milker units, the only part of the milker which needs to be moved, can readily be attached or detached. A portable milker is one in which the entire outfit, including power and pump, is carried, wheeled or transported on a cable from cow to cow. Why drag the entire milker about the barn twice a day, 365 days a year, when a few feet of pipe will eliminate this trouble forever?

13. **Sanitation.** No milker, regardless of how much time it may save, should be selected unless clean milk of high quality and low bacteria count can be produced with it. When the De Laval was designed this feature was kept in mind, so that it is easy to take apart and keep in a clean and sanitary condition. See page 21.

14. **Service.** The De Laval Milker requires less service than any other milker to begin with, and should any be required the De Laval Company is in a position to render quicker and better service than any other. See page 22.

15. **Cost.** In the long run, length and quality of service considered, a De Laval is the most economical milker and can be purchased on such easy terms that it will actually pay for itself while it is being used. See pages 9 and 22.

51

DeLaval

THE DE LAVAL MILKER

Milk produced in 1 year $2,410,000,000
Dairy cows required · 25,000,000
Amount of people required · 2,500,000
Actual hours of human labor · 5,000,000
At 15¢ per hour $750,000
for help   for one day

Time required to milk
a cow one year   — 133.9 hrs.
A De Laval milker will save
at least one half the time or — 62 hrs. per cow
@ 15¢ per hour - value of time saved — $9.30

(Average price of milk for 1922 was $2.20
per cwt. with average production of 5,000 lbs.
per cow and assuming a De Laval
milker increases production 10%)
value of extra milk produced   — $11.00

Total saving due to a De Laval — $20.30
Total saving on 10 cows   — $203.00
which is 6% interest on   — $3,383.00

DeLaval
picture from 1941 DeLaval
advertising booklet

DeLaval was one of the first to utilise
"Electronic" pulsation in their system.

DeLaval
picture from 1941 DeLaval advertising
booklet in Mike Gleason collection

DE LAVAL PORTABLE MILKERS

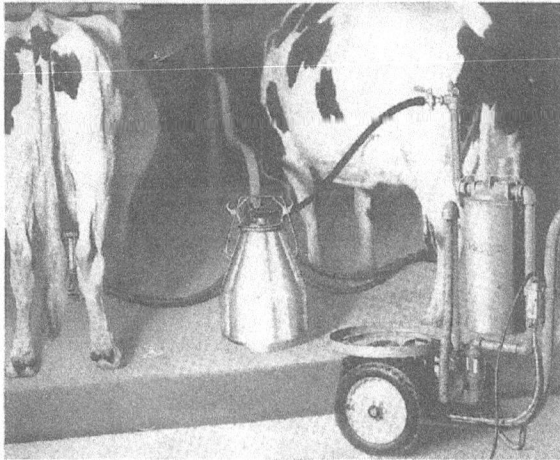

The De Laval Portable Milker is in every way the best outfit of its kind that has ever been offered to dairy farmers. It is compact, simple, very easy to handle, easy to keep in a clean and sanitary condition, and will milk cows better, faster and cleaner.

It comes to the user completely equipped for electrical connection and all ready to milk, and consists of a truck equipped with pneumatic rubber tires on which are mounted electric motor, vacuum pump and vacuum controller. It may be equipped with either a standard De Laval Milker of the Magnetic or Sterling type and with single or double unit, and will milk in exactly the same way as these De Laval Milkers. It has a ½-hp. motor and 25 feet of heavy cord with plug.

A De Laval Portable Milker can be quickly converted into a permanent pipe line installation whenever desired. Being standard equipment, the motor, vacuum pump and other parts may be removed from the truck, placed in a permanent setting and connected with pipe at very small expense. It is an advantage that every prospective user of a Portable should keep in mind—for some users may later desire this type of installation.

There are many uses for this De Laval Portable Milker. Aside from the dairyman who may not want to pipe up his barn for a permanent installation, there are many

dairies in which some cows may be milked in box stalls or in isolated barns, where a De Laval Portable can be used to good advantage. There are other sections of the country where at some times of the year cows are not milked in their barns.

Under such conditions cows can be milked anywhere an electrical connection can be made for this outfit.

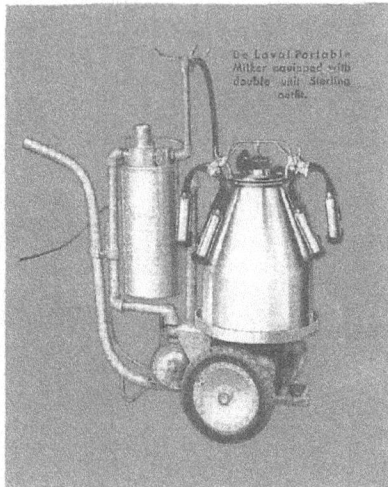

De Laval Portable Milker equipped with double unit Sterling outfit.

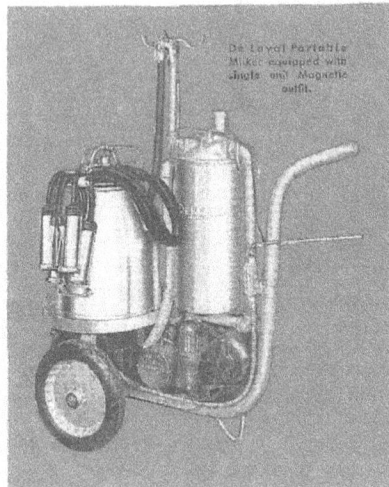

De Laval Portable Milker equipped with single unit Magnetic outfit.

[17]

DeLaval
Below are pictures of DeLaval milking
units in Mike Gleason collection

Delaval Aluminum 1927

Delaval Brass 1920

Delaval Galvanized

Delaval Double

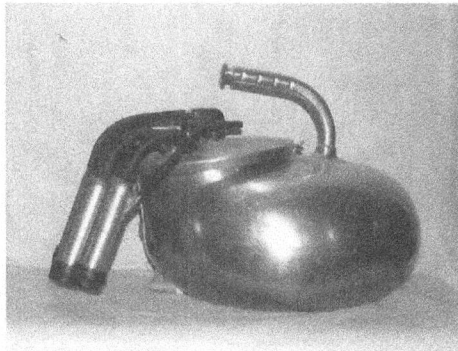

Disbrow Wonder Cow Milker

Northwestern Creamery Supply Company

Dept.. 5. St. Paul, MN

Hoard's Dairyman; February 11. 1916

Page 80

The Disbrow Wonder Cow Milker
better, cheaper and more reliable than the hired man. Write for full particulars and FREE descriptive booklet.
Northwestern Creamery Supply Co., Dept. 5, St. Paul, Minn.

Fort Atkinson Milker Company

Fort Atkinson. WI.

One reference is made in *1954 Implement Dealers Buyers Guide*. which says parts are no longer available. Nothing else is known.

Frosts Electric Milking Machine

This was sold by Sears in a catalog probably in the very early 1920s. None of these are known to exist. It is unknown who made them.

Some of the graphics in this book were copied from Dr. Paul Dettloff's book "Milking Machine Guide"

The Duplex Milker
Manufactured in Bath, NY Late 1930's or 1940's

Here's a rare one you collectors can start looking for in the graneries and sheets. A Duplex Milking Unit made in Bath, New York. Does anyone one?

THE DUPLEX
MILKS INTO A GLASS CHAMBER

ELECTRIC MODEL

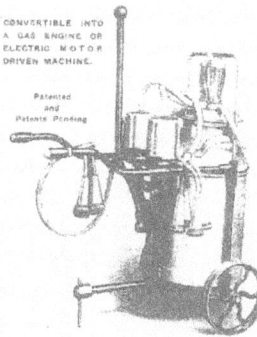

Front Cover Story

Use Duplex Portable
Milking Machines
For Visible Milking
and Sanitation

HAND POWER MODEL

CONVERTIBLE INTO
A GAS ENGINE OR
ELECTRIC MOTOR
DRIVEN MACHINE.

Patented
and
Patents Pending

The Duplex Milker
Manufactured in Bath, NY Late 1930's or
1940's

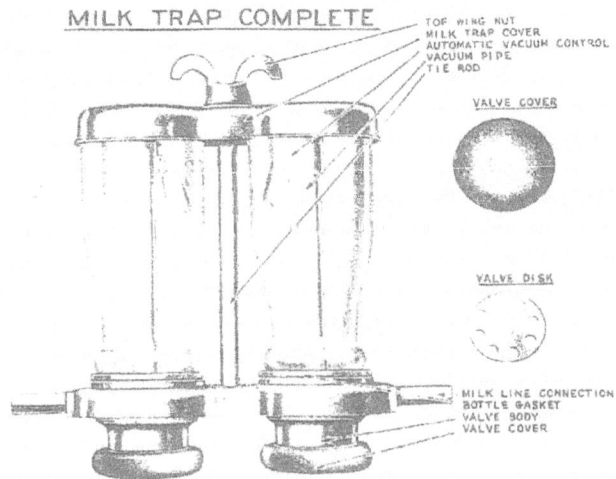

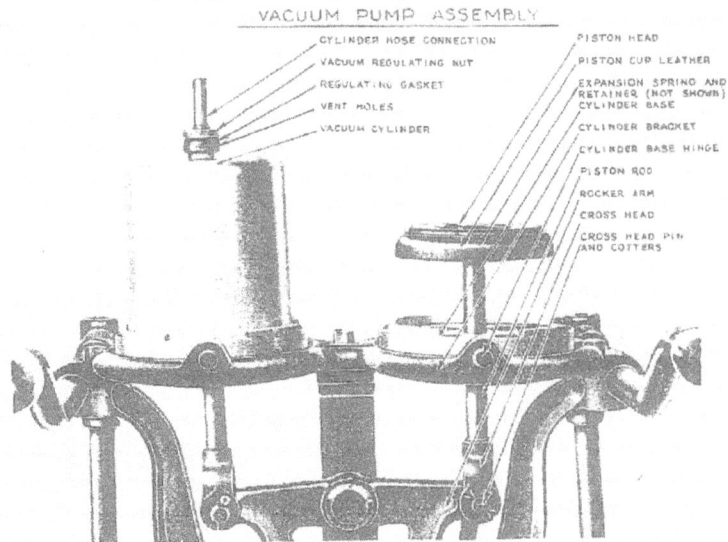

MILK TRAP COMPLETE

TOP WING NUT
MILK TRAP COVER
AUTOMATIC VACUUM CONTROL
VACUUM PIPE
TIE ROD

VALVE COVER

VALVE DISK

MILK LINE CONNECTION
BOTTLE GASKET
VALVE BODY
VALVE COVER

VACUUM PUMP ASSEMBLY

CYLINDER HOSE CONNECTION
VACUUM REGULATING NUT
REGULATING GASKET
VENT HOLES
VACUUM CYLINDER

PISTON HEAD
PISTON CUP LEATHER
EXPANSION SPRING AND
RETAINER (NOT SHOWN)
CYLINDER BASE
CYLINDER BRACKET
CYLINDER BASE HINGE
PISTON ROD
ROCKER ARM
CROSS HEAD
CROSS HEAD PIN
AND COTTERS

INSTRUCTIONS FOR ORDERING PARTS

Give Number and Name of Part ordered also Serial Number of Machine, togethe
r with type   that is Electric, Gas or Hand Power. All parts ordered are filled on a
strictly cash basis, to save the cost of opening small accounts.

WHERE REMITTANCE IS NOT RECEIVED WITH ORDER GOODS WILL
BE SENT C. O. D.

Empire Milker
Early 1900's
Bloomfield, NJ + Rochester, NY

This milker is one of 4 *Empires* in the Mike Gleason collection.

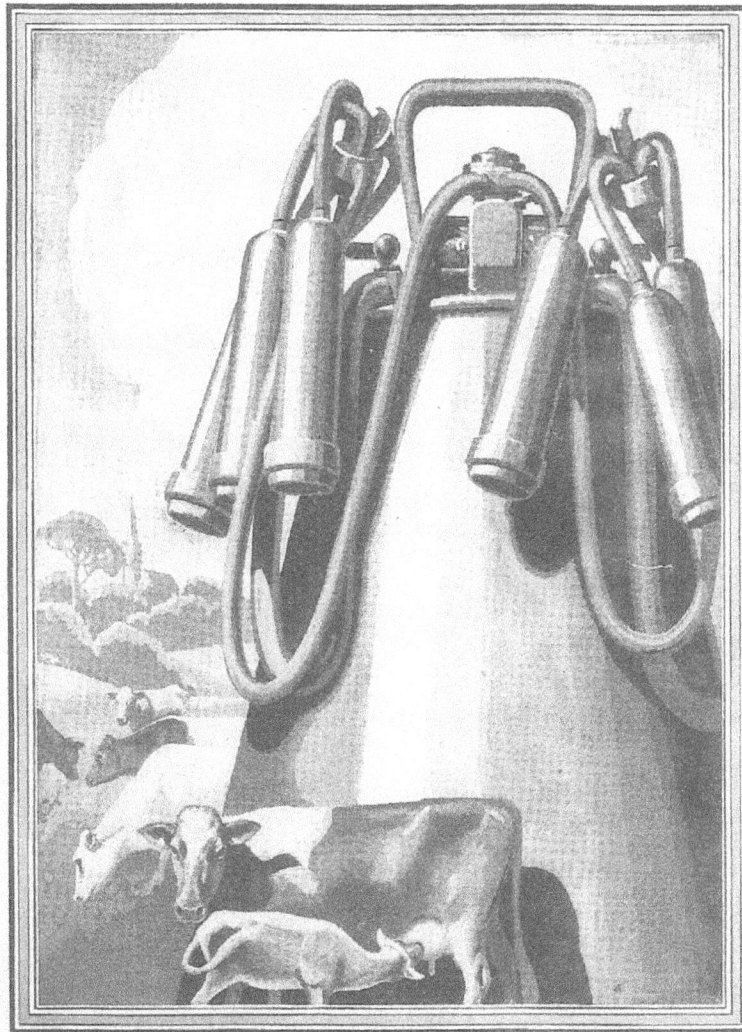

THE GREAT EMPIRE

From a 1928 Empire Milker manual in my collection

EMPIRE

Milks like the sucking calf

EMPIRE MILKING MACHINE COMPANY, INC.
97 Humboldt St., Rochester, N.Y.

Empire Milker
Early1900's
Bloomfield, NJ + Rochester, NY

ABOUT THE DAIRY COW

BEFORE we can intelligently consider the best methods of taking milk from a cow, we must know all we can about the cow and how she secretes and gives down milk. Unless every milking condition is recognized and proper provision is made for the comfort and health of the cow, the results are bound to be unsatisfactory.

In the design of the Empire Milking Machine, all guess work has been eliminated because the cow and her calf have been used as guides.

How the Cow Stores Milk—Every hour of the day the cow is making milk. The glands in the upper part of the udder are constantly at work storing up milk solids. At milking time these solids are mixed with water and pass through the milk channels to the milk reservoirs which are immediately over the teats.

Most of the milk is made while the cow is being milked. It is therefore, of the utmost importance that nothing must be allowed to irritate, excite, or fret the cow at this time. Any of these things cause her to hold back her milk, make it harder to get, cause her to make less milk.

In many successful dairies it is the rule that for an hour previous to milking, the cows must have perfect quiet, no loud talking or anything to disturb or excite them. While the cows are being milked the same rules are observed and no roughness in milking or handling the cows is tolerated.

A Delicate Mechanism—The modern dairy cow is a delicate, nervous animal. She is easily upset—especially when any unusual strain is put upon her udder or when there is even slight teat irritation. The teats are extremely sensitive. They are easily injured. Even when the same person milks a cow every day, by hand, she is likely to be restive and uncomfortable when the milking begins. With a stranger on the milking stool few cows will keep up to their standard production. For best results, milking must be regular, uniform and comfortable—almost impossible when milking is done by hand, because after milking a few cows the hands become tired and often the milker's temper becomes frayed. Or he is in a hurry to get the chore done and is likely to be a bit rough.

How Should a Cow be Milked—The calf is the world's champion milker. Hands and machines can only imitate the calf's method. Hand milking is much further away from the natural calf style of milking than the Empire way which recreates the sucking and massage action of the calf so perfectly that heifers and even old cows have been observed licking the Empire pail just as they would lick their calves. Milking should be so comfortable that it does not disturb the cow. During milking cows continue to contentedly chew their cuds when Empire Milkers are used. They have been known to try and lie down while milking was going on. When it comes to the question of suiting the cow, there is no doubt about where the Empire Milker stands.

[5]

From a 1928 Empire Milker manual in my collection

Empire Milker
Early 1900's
Bloomfield, NJ + Rochester, NY

Alternate Milking or All Teats at Once—If men had four hands, no question would ever have been raised as to how many teats to milk at one time. If it were easier to milk two teats in unison instead of alternately, which gives each hand a little rest and allows the milker to focus his attention on the hand which is giving the pressure, that would have become the accepted method.

As it stands, we have only two hands and it is easier and more comfortable to milk in rhythm, first one hand and then the other. So many have come to look upon this as the natural, normal way.

Let the Cow Decide—The cow can't talk but let us see what she might say. In the first place she secretes milk in all four quarters of her udder at one time and lets it down as soon as secreted. If only one teat is being milked the weight of the milk let down to the other teats soon distresses a cow unless it is drawn away. It puts a strain on the udder muscles and supports (mammary muscles) which is bad for the cow. When the calf milks he frequently switches from teat to teat and relieves this strain.

With hand milking this switching around is imperfectly accomplished. Two teats are milked and then the other two. Then all the teats are stripped dry.

Using the Empire Milker, all the teats are milked at once. As fast as the cow lets down her milk it is drawn away from all four quarters of the udder. There is no unnecessary strain put on the mammary muscles. The time taken to produce and get rid of the milk is less than by any other method. Conse-

quently, the strain on the cow is less. To put it another way, she has the strength and energy to put into producing which is wasted by a longer, slower method of milking. That this is not mere theory is abundantly proved by hundreds of letters from Empire users which tell of increased daily milk production and longer lactation periods when Empire Milking was substituted for hand milking.

Easy Milkers and Hard Milkers—But you say all cows are not alike. Some are easy milkers and some are hard milkers. Some have small teats and some have large teats. Cows with three teats are not uncommon. The teat pattern on the udder varies. Some cows have one or two large teats and the others much smaller. Cows are not built to any set standard.

All these things are true. They were all considered. They are all provided for in the Empire Milker. Otherwise, we could not ask a practical dairy farmer to think of investing a dollar of his hard-earned cash in a machine which would only work on a few of his cows and actually cost him more in time, labor and money than hand milking.

Like a Sucking Calf—To say that the Empire milks like a sucking calf, is a broad statement but it is literally true. As the calf takes the teat into its mouth the teat is massaged from tip to udder. Then the calf sucks to draw the milk. As its mouth fills, the suction is released while the milk is swallowed. This allows the blood drawn toward the end of the teat by suction to flow back to the udder. The three-way massage of the teat by the

[6]

From a 1928 Empire Milker manual in my collection

Empire Milker
Early1900's
Bloomfield, NJ + Rochester, NY

calf's tongue and the roof of its mouth beginning at the tip of the teat and going up to the udder stimulates this return of the blood to the udder before the calf again sucks more milk into the mouth.

How exactly this calf-milking is recreated by the patented Empire Teat Cup is explained in detail on page 14. It illustrates how accurately nature's model milker has been studied and copied in the making of the Empire Milker.

What Suits the Cow Benefits the Owner—Over twenty years of successful milking of all breeds and types of cows by the Empire Milker is the best kind of evidence. Scores of letters written by owners of Empire Milking Machines, who have used them continuously for periods ranging from a few months to seventeen years, indicate the settled conviction of progressive dairy farmers that this milker meets every requirement of the dairy cow and its owner.

The letters from Empire users, which we are including in this book, tell just what their experience has been. They indicate what you may expect when the Empire goes to work for you—quicker milking at less cost of time and labor—more milk per cow—longer lactation period—less teat and udder trouble—bigger profits from your present herd—an opportunity to build up your herd without building up labor costs.

Read these letters carefully. Consult any neighbor who has an Empire Milker. Ask the nearest Empire dealer for a demonstration and for the liberal credit arrangement that permits you to take immediate advantage of the economies of Empire Milking and allows you all the time you need to pay for this perfected method of milking.

[7]

From a 1928 Empire Milker manual in my collection

63

Empire Milker
Early1900's
Bloomfield, NJ + Rochester, NY

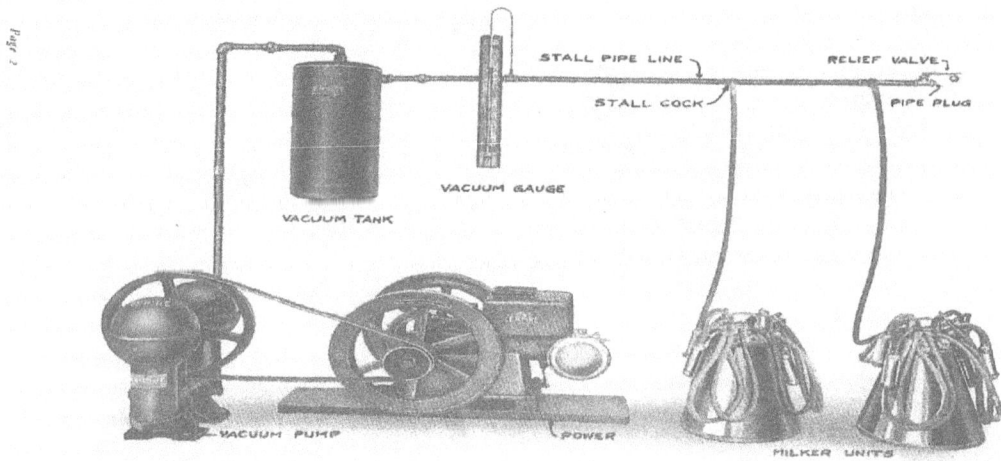

STALL PIPE LINE
RELIEF VALVE
STALL COCK
PIPE PLUG
VACUUM GAUGE
VACUUM TANK
VACUUM PUMP
POWER
MILKER UNITS

Illustration No. 2
This illustration shows the correct placing of the Empire Pump, Vacuum Tank, Vacuum Gauge and Relief Valve.

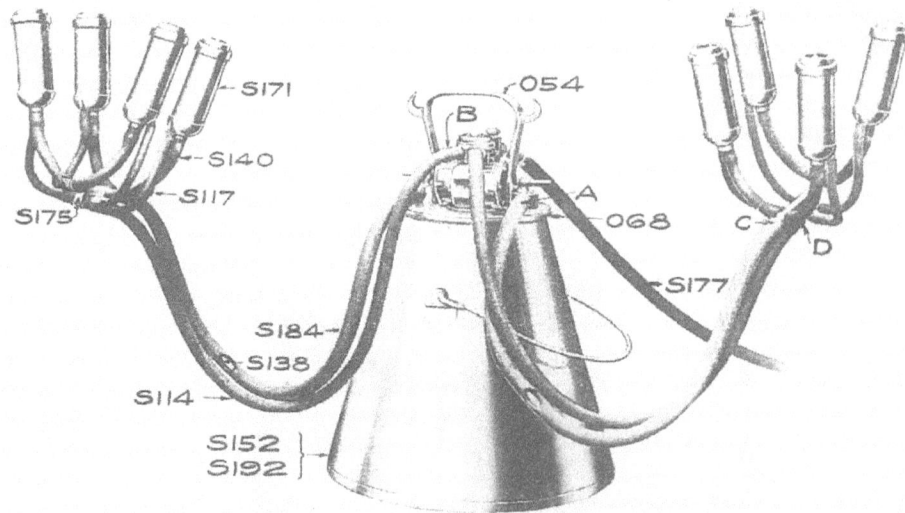

S171
S140
S117
S175
054
B
A
068
C
D
S177
S184
S138
S114
S152
S192

Illustration No. 6

Page 6

From a 1921 Empire Milker manual in my collection

Ever-Ready Portable Milker

Dairy Supply Company
381 Fourth Ave
New York 16, NY

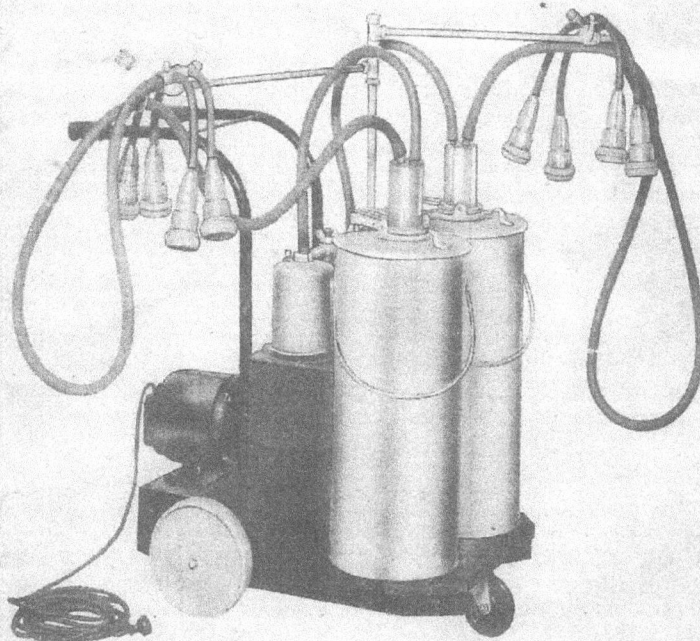

How to Use
The "EVER-READY" Portable Milker

Complete Instructions for Setting up
and Operating the Machine, including
Important Information concerning its
care and cleaning, together with—

Price List for Parts

DAIRY SUPPLY COMPANY
381 Fourth Ave.   New York 16, N. Y.

From a 1931 Manual in my collection of reference materials.

Ever-Ready Portable Milker

Dairy Supply Company
381 Fourth Ave
New York 16, NY

COWS ARE CREATURES OF HABIT. Every dairy farmer knows this. That is why cows must be taught, or trained, to respond properly to a milking machine. No machine made can milk every cow in every herd completely dry,— although the EVER-READY has done so on some herds. Nor can any milking machine take the milk from a cow any faster than she is willing to let it down. No machine can pull the milk from a cow if she is not willing to permit it. If you have any obstinate cows, let them become accustomed to the machine gradually.

2. About Milking:

a. No machine can take the milk from a cow if she is not willing to give it down. Many cows do not become accustomed to milking machines simply because they have not been properly trained at the beginning. By using the following method, you will make sure that you are not losing any milk while you are training a cow; also, you will make sure that your cow is properly trained—and adjusted—to the use of a milking machine.

DO NOT LEAVE THE MILKING MACHINE ON THE COWS ANY LONGER THAN 3 MINUTES DURING THE FIRST 7 DAYS. Regardless of how the cow reacts to the machine during that period, take the milking machine off the cow at the end of three minutes. If at the end of three minutes she has not let down her milk, or has only partially done so, remove the machine and finish milking her by hand. If this Three-Minute Principle is carried out morning and night for SEVEN consecutive days, you will find your cows are properly broken in to the use of the milking machine.

b. To obtain the best results after the cow has thus been properly trained, especially from the standpoint of sanitation and correct milking, you should prepare the cow for milking by using a clean cloth dipped into hot water—130 to 140 degrees, F.—containing a little chlorine disinfectant, such as B-K. With this solution, wash and massage the cows' udder and teats thoroughly for about five to ten seconds. This will cause the cow to give down her milk more readily than any other method that is known.

Just before attaching the teat cups, strip a little milk from each teat to wash away the bacteria formation which usually gathers at the end of the teat. This will also enable you to inspect each teat for cuts and sores. Never wash the udder and teats of a cow until you are ready to milk her. Otherwise, you lose the benefit of the hot-water massage.

From a 1931 Manual in my collection of reference materials.

Ever-Ready Portable Milker

Dairy Supply Company
381 Fourth Ave
New York 16, NY

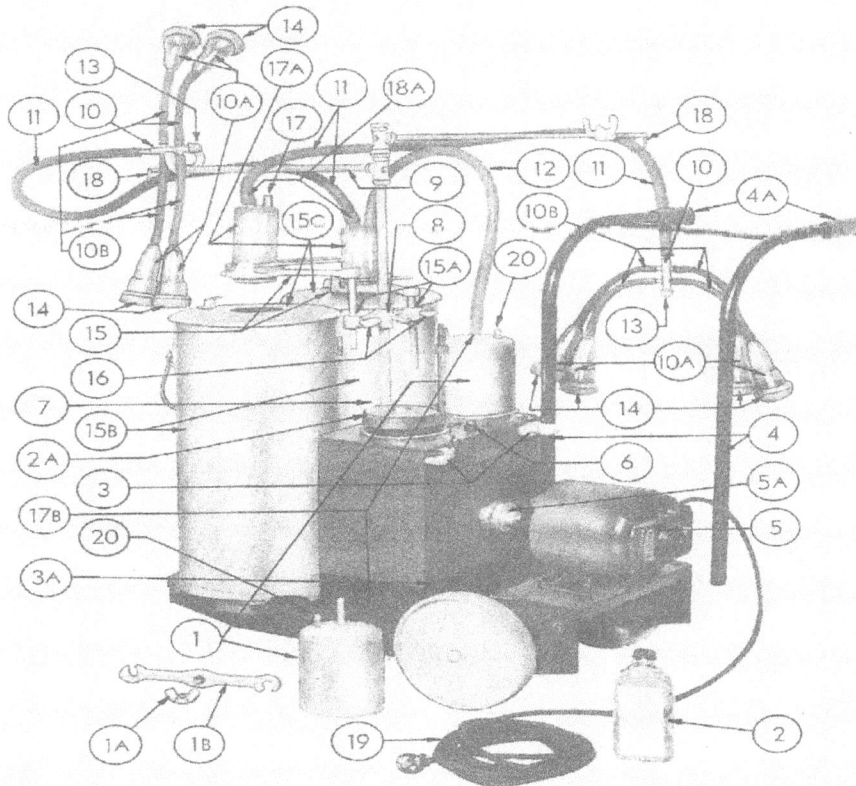

EXPLANATORY DETAIL OF ILLUSTRATION

1. Vacuum Cylinder. (One Cylinder removed to show Piston Head. (2-a)
1a. Winged Nut, and (1-b) Clamp for holding Cylinders in place.
2. 8 Oz. Bottle of Neatsfoot Oil for lubricating Cylinders.
2a. Piston Head, equipped with compressor leather.
3. Clamps for holding Handle Bars.
3a. Studs on chassis over which Handle Bars fit.
4. Handle Bars.
4a. Rubber Grips on Handle Bars.
5. ¼ H. P. Motor.
5a. Flexible Coupling between Motor and Worm Gear.
6. Plug at top of Chassis, to be removed when putting in oil.
7. Set-Screw for holding Milk Line Arm Assembly.

8. Saddle for holding Milk Chamber Assembly.
9. Standard and Arms for supporting Milk Line Assembly.
10. Four-Prong Claws.
10a. Transparent Plastic Teat Cups.
10b. Short Milk Lines (7 in.)
11. Main Milk Line (6 ft. long) in two pieces with metal connection.
12. Vacuum Line connecting Cylinders with Milk Chambers. (One Vacuum Line removed. See 17)
13. Caps covering top ends of Claws.
14. Rubber Caps, or Cushions, on Teat Cups.
15. Milk Head Chamber Assembly for holding Milk Chambers firmly to top of Milk Cans.

15a. Hole in Saddle (8) for inserting Milk Head Assembly.
15b. Milk Cans, 19½ Qt. Capacity.
15c. Covers on Milk Cans.
16. Thumb Screws for holding Milk Head Assembly in place.
17. Connection on Milk Chamber for Vacuum Line.
17a. Transparent Plastic Milk Chambers.
17b. Connection at top of Cylinder for attaching Vacuum Line.
18. Rings on Milk Line Assembly Arm for supporting Main Milk Lines.
18a. Slanting connection at top of Milk Chamber for connecting Main Milk Lines.
19. 16-ft. Electric Cord.
20. Thumb Screws at top of Cylinders for regulating Vacuum Control.

9

From a 1931 Manual in my collection of reference materials.

Fairbanks-MorseAutomatic Milking Machine
Chicago, ILL.
1931

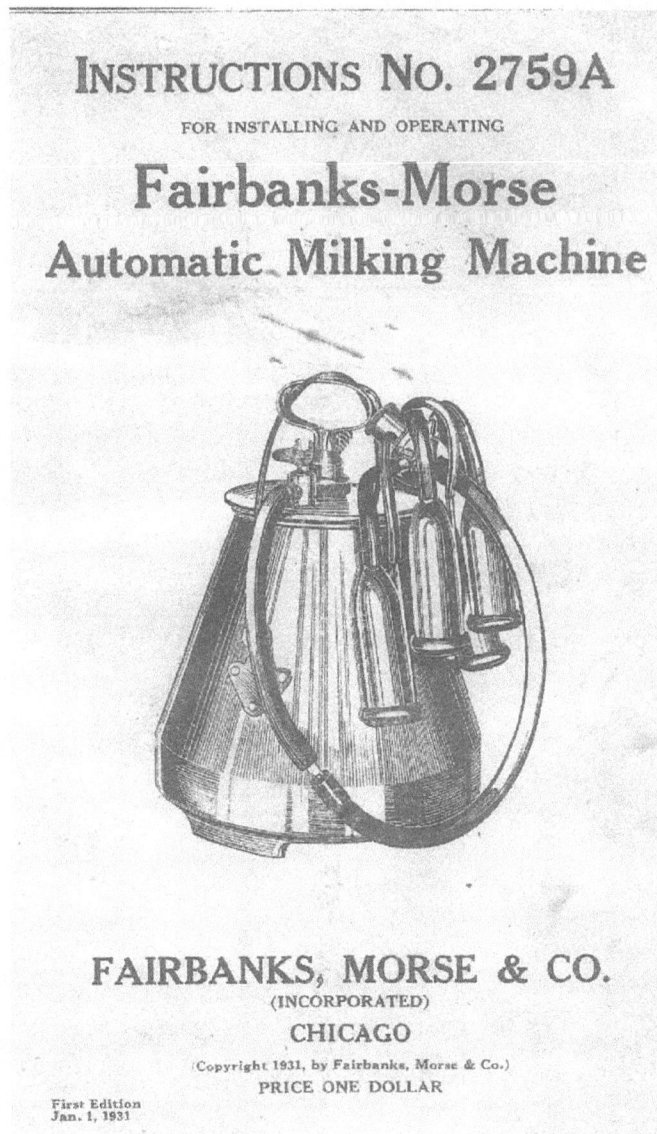

INSTRUCTIONS No. 2759A

FOR INSTALLING AND OPERATING

Fairbanks-Morse
Automatic Milking Machine

FAIRBANKS, MORSE & CO.
(INCORPORATED)
CHICAGO
(Copyright 1931, by Fairbanks, Morse & Co.)
PRICE ONE DOLLAR

First Edition
Jan. 1, 1931

1931 manual in my collection

Fairbanks-MorseAutomatic Milking Machine
Chicago, ILL.
1931

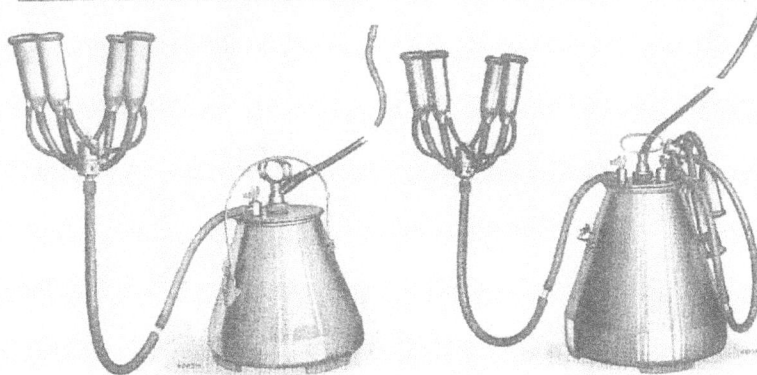

Figure 13. Single Unit

Figure 14. Double Unit

II. OPERATING INSTRUCTIONS

1. ASSEMBLING THE UNITS

Before assembling the units, rinse all rubber parts in warm water and brush the inside of teat-cup shells free from dust and packing material.

In assembling the teat-cups, the inflation (teat-cup liner) should be drawn into the shell until the large rubber bead at the top presses against the rim of the shell; the bead should then be snapped over the shell rim. (See Figs. 15 and 16.) Next screw pulsator into teat-cup claw (See Fig. 17); attach teat-cups to pulsator and claw, and attach milk tube to claw.

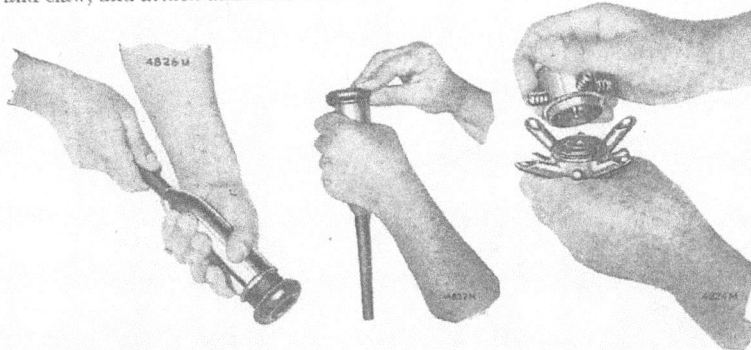

Figure 15.
Assembling Teat-Cups

Figure 16.
Snapping Bead
over Shell Rim

Figure 17.
Assembling Pulsator
on Teat-Cup Claw

1931 manual in my collection

Fairbanks-MorseAutomatic Milking Machine
Chicago, ILL.
1931

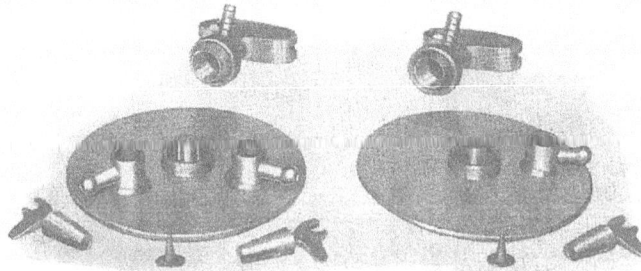

Figure 18.   Double and Single Unit Pail Covers Disassembled

2. TESTING THE UNITS

To test the unit, start the vacuum pump and see that the gauge registers between 12 and 13 on the dial. Attach the free end of the black stanchion hose to a stallcock and with the milk spigot on the pail closed, turn on the vacuum at the stallcock. This will draw the cover tight on the pail; any hissing of air at the cover edge will indicate that it is not assembled correctly.

Now hold the teat-cup cluster with the pulsator upright and all cups hanging straight down. (See Fig. 19.) Open milk spigot on pail cover and pulsator will commence to function, making a clicking sound. It should run at a rate of about 110 clicks per minute; this can be regulated by turning thumbscrew on side of pulsator. (See Fig. 20.)

Insert a thumb in one of the cups and hold it with thumb pointing down. (See Fig. 21.) The teat-cup liner (the inflation) alternately squeezes and releases the

Figure 19. Holding Teat-Cup Cluster
to Shut Off Vacuum on Cups

Figure 20. Regulating Speed
of Pulsator

1931 manual in my collection

Fords Milker
mid 1920's
Sold by Myers-Sherman Company
215 Deplaines St.
Chicago, ILL.

Fords

The above milker
in color is in the
Mike Gleason
milker collection

— NEW IMPROVED —

Fords Milker

Gas Engine and Electric Types

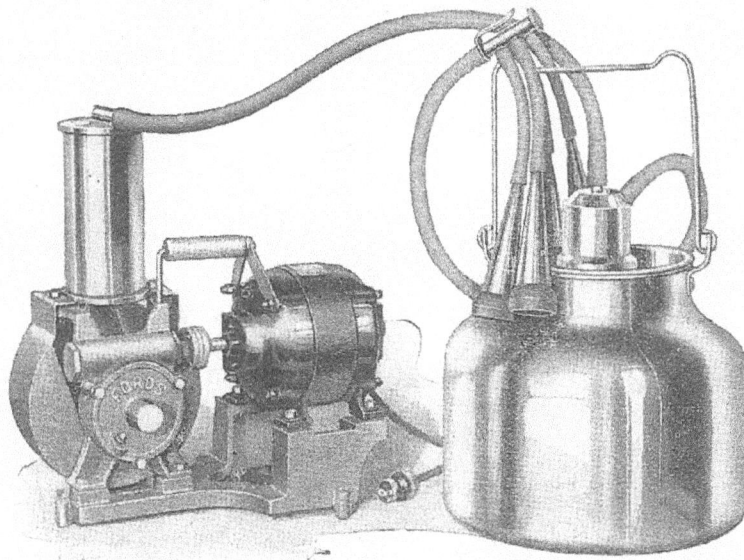

Lowest Priced Power Milker **$100**⁰⁰
Single Unit

QUALITY GUARANTEED

The greatest and most substantial value in
power milking machines.
Read What Users Say

From a 1927 Fords Milker Advertizement booklet in my collection.

Fords Milker
mid 1920's
Sold by Myers-Sherman Company
215 Deplaines St.
Chicago, ILL.

Fords Double Single Electric
WITH CARRIER
$180.00
Fords Double Double Electric
$250.00

Fords Double Single Electric Milker combines two single units and operates them with the same power plant. It is designed to milk two cows at a time into separate containers.

Fords Double Double Electric Milker combines two double units, and operates them with the same power plant. It is the same construction except that pumps and pails are larger. Two cows are milked into each pail.

"DOES BETTER WORK — LASTS LONGER — AND COSTS LESS"

From a 1927 Fords Milker Advertizement booklet in my collection.

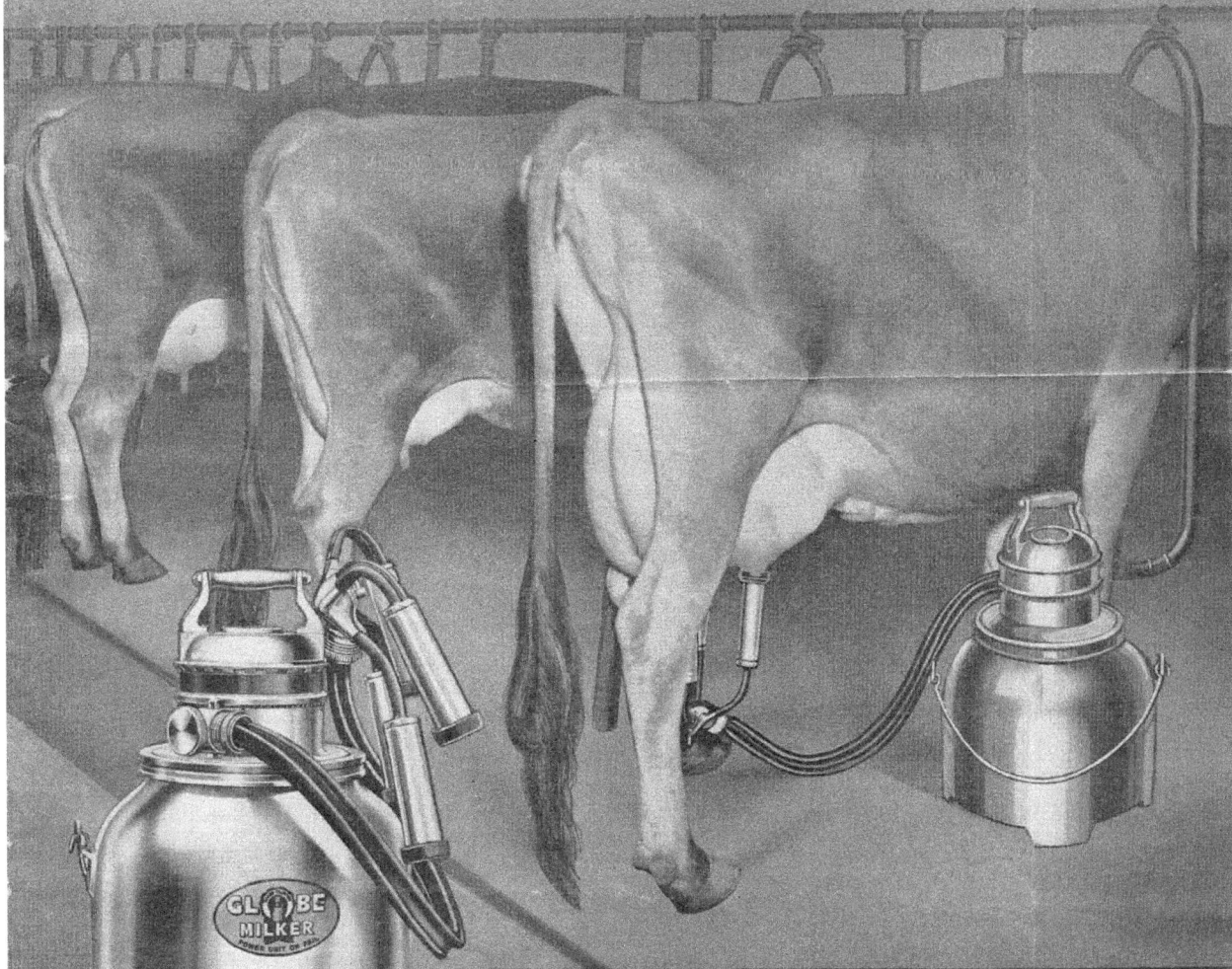

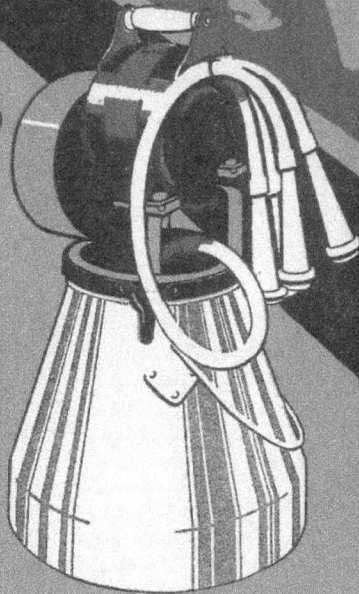

Hinman Milker
Invented 1906-07 by A. V. and R. L. Hinman, father and son in Oneida, NY

The Milking Machine

THE profits of the modern farmer and dairyman depend upon the employment of labor- and time-saving machinery.

His success consists in letting the machine perform the labor formerly executed by hand whenever the machine can do the work more quickly, more efficiently and at a lower cost.

This rule applies to milking cows and it seems strange that many farmers who long ago substituted the mowing machine for the scythe and the threshing machine for the flail are still milking their cows in the same way as did their ancestors, although for six years milking machines have done perfect work.

Milking machines are not designed for the rich only, but are within the reach of every farmer who has a dairy of ten cows or more. The machine has become a recognized part of the equipment of large dairies throughout the world. It is much nearer the *natural* process than is the hand method. The flow of milk is more even and all dairy experts agree that the more uniformly the cows are milked the greater and more regular will be the flow of milk. For this reason a good hand milker "gets more milk" than a poor milker.

Users of the milking machine know that the machines save an almost unbelievable portion of labor over hand milking; that it is much cleaner and more satisfactory in every way. With the machine there are no udder troubles or sore teats—and that is more than can be said of hand milking. It is a recognized fact that the cows like the machine much better than the hand method, and, unlike the latter, the machine is gentle, regular, steady and cannot hurt or excite the cows. A correspondent to farm publications states that there is no other machine that can be put on a dairy farm that will pay for itself as quickly in saving time and work as will the milking machine.

3

From a 1914 Hinman Milker manual in my collection

Hinman Electric Milker
late 1930's to mid 1940's.

A daring concept making vacum pump all in one piece
From a manual in Mike Gleason collection

from a Hoegger Supply Company brochure

Hoegger Supply Company

Milford, PA.

Hoegger Supply Company marketed a unique goat milker.

from a Hoegger Supply Company brochure

Hoover Milker Company

One reference is made in the *1953 Implement Buyer's Guide.* Nothing else is known.

This page compiled from advertising graphics in Paul Dettloff book "Milking Machine Guide"

Marlow Milker
established 1947

Marlow Milker 1960

Marlow milker in
Mike Gleason
collection.
Located in
Herkimer, NY

J. C. MARLOW
The Pioneer in Milkers

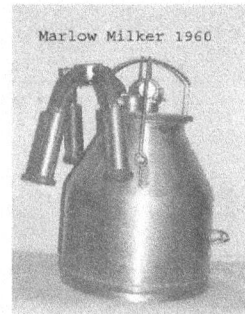

43 Years a Milker Man

J. C. says: "Way back in 1908, I traveled 60 miles to see the first milking machine operating in Wisconsin. When I saw a boy and a girl, 10 and 12 years old, milk 20 cows in one hour, I decided immediately to buy one . . . and I've actually *lived* milkers ever since. I was so impressed with the results I got that I invited my neighbors in to see it operate. They asked me to order machines for them . . . and the first thing I knew I was in the milking machine business.

"Selling milkers was pioneer work 43 years ago. Dairymen were skeptical about machines . . . especially machines that worked on a live subject. But I was quite successful because I knew cows and milking as a practical dairyman and I knew my machine would make dairying easier. So I traveled through snow, mud and rain by horse and buggy, and later by Model T Ford, to help dairymen solve their milking problems.

"Later, my wife and I organized our own distributing agency, and because we always gave the best service possible, it became one of the largest agencies in the country. For

This page compiled from advertising graphics in pall order book "Milking Machine Guide"

Marlow Milker
established 1947

THE MARLOW WAS DEVELOPED BY A PRACTICAL DAIRYMAN ON HIS OWN PUREBRED HERDS

Long before the Marlow Milker was introduced to the public, it was carefully developed, tested and proved on J. C. Marlow's own purebred Holstein herds.

J. C. knew his cows and milker, so his first big objective was to protect those cows by eliminating the major cause of mastitis and udder troubles, due to improper milking and machines which crawled up and "swallowed" the udder, bruising the tender tissues. The Marlow Milker, then, was designed to operate, not with irritating high vacuum, but with *low vacuum* at a high pulsation rate (up to 120 per minute). These developments, plus special built-in features, keep teats and udders healthy by stimulating the cow's blood flow to the udder, and increasing the cow's ability to "manufacture" more milk. And since a healthy-uddered cow stays in the herd longer, her lifetime profit to the dairyman is substantially increased, and her re-sale value is also higher.

Another big objective was to increase milk production by building a milker that cows *liked*. He found that cows responded best to a low vacuum milker with a gentle, soothing, vigorous massaging action. This caused the cows to keep pressure on the udder during milking, forcing that last and richest milk from the top of the udder down into the teat cisterns and then into the pail. He also proved that cows held up longer on lactations, due to this action, resulting in greatly increased dairy profits.

The fact that the Marlow definitely increases production and stops the major cause of mastitis is proved by the outstanding records of the two Marlow herds. Recently classified, No. 1 Farm had 81.3 points and No. 2 had 81.4 points. All cows on test are Marlow-milked twice daily, running with the herd with no special care, and records up to 919.6 lbs. fat have been made in 10 months on twice-a-day milking. You are invited to write for additional information and will be welcome to visit our farms at any time.

Oostie Femco Alma Ideal, Marlow's own National Champion Cow, daughter of Femco Almas Only-Son on July 26, 1951 completed a Ten Month's Record of 919.60 lbs. fat, 4.90% test, 18,957 lbs. milk, twice-a-day milking. Freshened again in just 29 days. Off to another great start — first 35 days 142.30 lbs. fat — over 4 lbs. per day.

DIFFERENT because of its RESULTS!

Hundreds of letters — from dairymen all across the country — prove the Marlow is different because of the results it delivers. If you want increased milk production, healthier teats and udders for your cows, longer herd life, and longer lactations . . . if you milk cows for maximum profits — *then it will pay you to switch to Marlow Milkers!* Ask any Marlow user!

From reference material in Mike Gleason collection

McCormick-Deering
Manufactured by The International Harvester Company
Chicago, ILL
early 1930's until early1950's

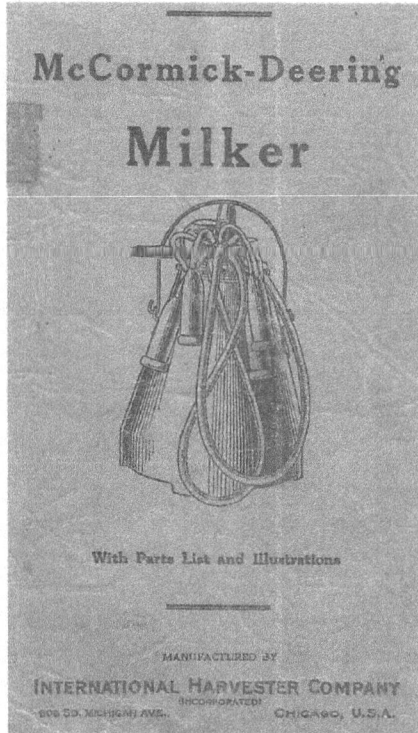

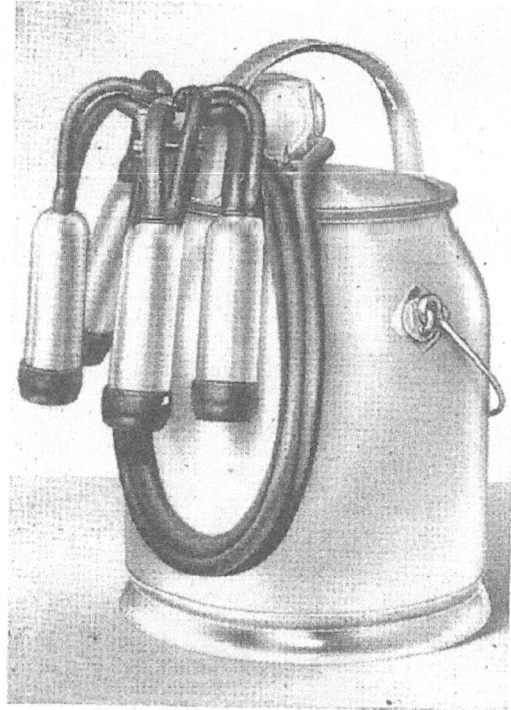

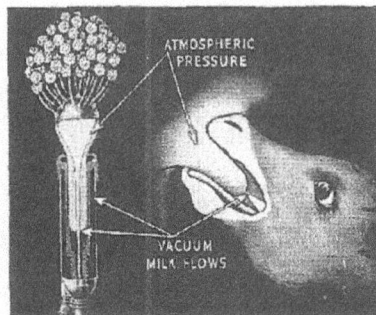

Illust. 22

The calf and the mechanical milker both apply vacuum to obtain milk.

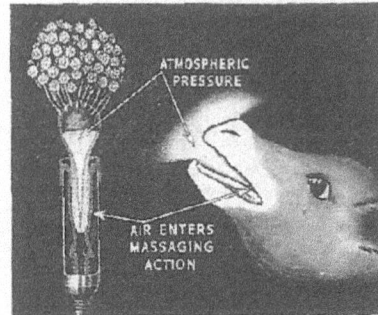

Illust. 23

Air is released into the space between the teat cup shell and the inflation to squeeze the teat.

Mehring
Invented and sold byWm. M Mehring
York Road, Carrol Co. MD.
Mr. Merhing is known for two milking units, the "Mehring Hand Powered Milker" and the "Mehring Foot Power Milker".
Both are pictured below.

Mehring's Pneumatic Hand Power COW MILKER.

This is his first successful milker. It was first patented in 1892. It is no longer being manufactured, as the Foot Power, needing but one person, has taken its place.

A pail should be hung on the pump spout. A boy or girl pumps, and another puts the cups on the cow.

MEHRING'S FOOT POWER COW MILKER.

WM. M. MEHRING.

✎TERMS.✎

The retail price of the milker for two cows is $75 on time or $70 for cash. For places west of the Mississippi river, the cost of the freight is added. Where we have no agents, we make the farmer pay in advance, part of the traveling expenses of the agent who sets up the machine. The charge will be from $5 to $10. If you state your locality, we will then tell you exactly what it will cost to start a machine. Then if you buy, we will sell to you for the same price as to an agent.

We also deduct the amount you paid for setting up the Machine from the wholesale price. If you do not buy, we keep what was paid for traveling expenses. When the distance is too great we refuse to send an agent. But will sell to the farmer for cash, and let him undertake to learn to operate the machine himself. We send two large direction circulars showing how to operate the machine. As to my responsibility, I refer you to LeGore Banking Co., Le-Gore, Md.   WM. M. MEHRING,
                                        YORK ROAD, MD.

The milking unit pictured below is in personal milking machine collection of Mike Gleason, Herkimer, NY

Mehring 1895

Mehring
Invented and sold byWm. M Mehring
York Road, Carrol Co MD
Mr. Merhing is known for two milking units, the "Mehring Hand Powered Milker" and the "Mehring Foot Power Milker"
Both are pictured below.

This cut shows how to keep the machine after milking. The round arm extending from under the spigot of pump, is the handle by which the machine is carried.

The little forked iron, on the opposite side from the handle is to keep the pail from swinging.

The fixtures on the wall are, reading from left to right: Hose Swab, Hair Swab for Teat Cups &c. Hair Swab for small tubing, Wrench, Hose, Teat Cups, and soft rubber disks. There are 3 glass sections hanging on the string with the disks, but they can not be seen in the cut.

The disks are for repairs, and they are not removed from the cups unless they are worn out.

When writing for a machine, tell all about your dairy. the breed you keep, if you run a summer or winter dairy, what use is made of the milk, if you raise or buy your cows, if you help to milk personally. Also give your county and nearest railroad station.

For further particulars address the agent,

Or enclose stamp to the manufacturer, W. M. MEHRING, York Road, Carroll Co., Maryland

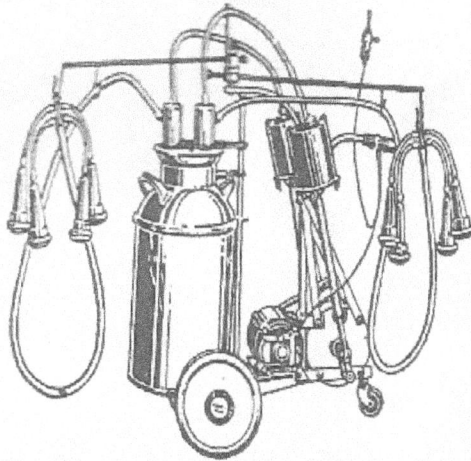

Milking Can Be A LIGHT Chore Now!

2. Milking Machines have no brain—and cows cannot talk. Sometimes when trouble comes it taxes the ingenuity of the operator to determine just what the cause is. It is not always just what you at first think it is.

The above pictures and quote are taken from an early 1940's advertising flyer in Mike Gleason collection

PERFECTION MILKERS

HOW MUCH SUCTION IS REQUIRED TO MILK A COW ?

Perfection Milking Machine

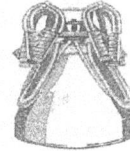

THAT'S WHAT THEY SAID

Milking Machine? You're Either a Crook or Crazy

WHEN LAURITS DINESEN was a young man in Denmark, in 1899, the women milkers on his brother-in-law's farm went on strike.

"My brother-in-law had to do the milking then," 67-year-old Dinesen recalled today at the Minnesota State fair. "So he asked me, 'Why don't you invent a milking machine?' "

Dinesen had already built a windmill to supply electric power; he thought the idea of a milking machine was a good one and set to work making one. Today he is chairman of the board and research director of the Perfection Manufacturing Corp., 2125 E. Hennepin avenue, a firm doing $2,000,000 in business yearly.

The first models of Dinesen's milking machines, differing greatly in appearance but operating on the same principles as the sleek modern ones, are on display at the firm's booth at the fair's Dairy building.

Dinesen remembers that his first models were hand-operated. Others employed water wheels, and one milker was attached to the cow while a horse turning a windlass supplied the power.

Setting up shop in a corner of his father's woodworking factory at Vejle, Dinesen sold 25 of his first models and 50 of the second.

"But I couldn't compete with the cheap labor of the women milkers," Dinesen said.

He emigrated to Minneapolis in 1912 and, attending the state fair the following year, saw other makes of milking machines.

"They didn't look as good as ...ne, so I borrowed $250 and ...nt into business," he said.

Dinesen's first place of busi...ss was on old grocery store on ...anklin avenue; his second a ...mer saloon at Twenty-sixth ...eet and Twenty-sixth avenue

He had started a stock com...ny, and in 1917 built the pres...t plant.

...elling milking machines wasn't ...sy in the early days, he re...mbers.

When he set up his first exhibit ...the West hotel, he was unable ...speak English and had to hire ...neone to sell his wares.

'People thought someone trying ...sell a milking machine was ...her a crook or crazy," he said.

One time, when he was at a ...me at Eden Prairie, Dinesen ...erheard the woman of the house ...ing: "He seems to be a nice ...n. Too bad he's a little off."

'Now I'm selling machines to ...e sons in that family," he said. Dinesen went to Denmark last ...ar and found the early models ...the machine in his brother-in-...v's attic.

LAURITS DINESEN AND HIS FIRST MILKING MACHINE
A modern model in the background

★ ★ ★ ★   ★ ★ ★ ★

THAT'S WHAT THEY SAID

Milking Machine? You're Either a Crook or Crazy

This is a clipping from a 1949 Minnesota newspaper about Mr. Dineson and the Perfection Milking Machine.

PERFECTION
MANUFACTURING COMPANY
MANUFACTURERS OF
PERFECTION MILKERS
VACUUM PUMPS AND AIR COMPRESSORS

MINNEAPOLIS, MINN. Mar. 22, 1919

MADE IN DENMARK -1909-

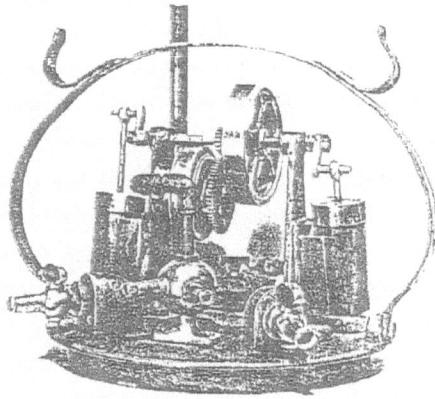

This is a clipping from a 1949 Minnesota newspaper about Mr. Diensen and the Perfection Milking Machine.

The first Milking Machine built by Mr. Dinesen is now in the Danish Museun located in Elkhorn, Iowa

Perfection 1926

Perfection Auto 1932

Perfection 1935-40

Prima Milker

Mfg by Rite-way but sold under Sears-Roebuck name Rite-Way Milker was a sub Company of the Massey-Harris Company,Limited. Massy-Harris was established in1847.

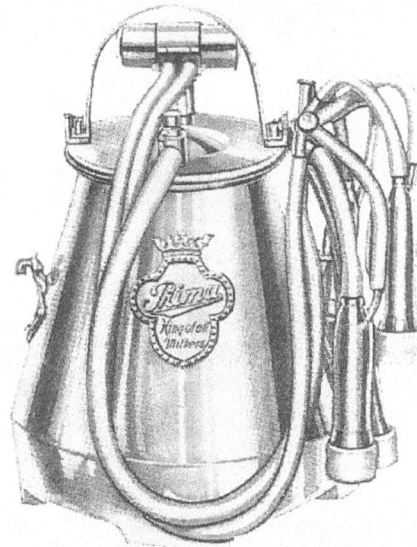

Single Unit

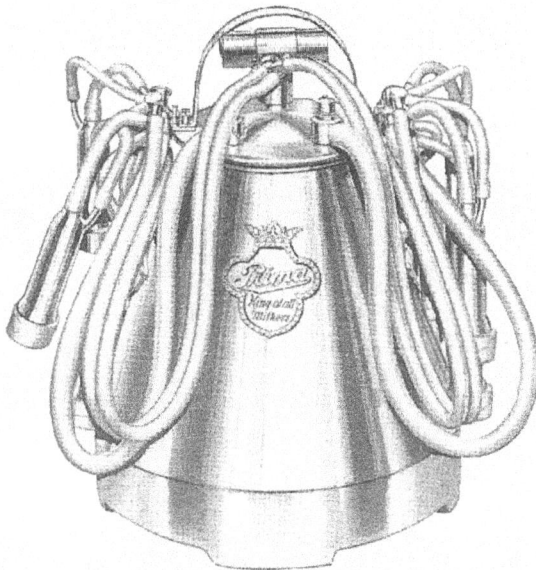

Double Unit

Much conjecture as to who made Sears-Roebuck and Montgomery-Ward Milker. In 1950's all three used the same claw and pulsators. The swing unit came on the market in late 1940's as Rite-Ways answer to the Surge belly milker.
The above pictures are from the Mike Gleason milker manual collection

The Milker Magazine

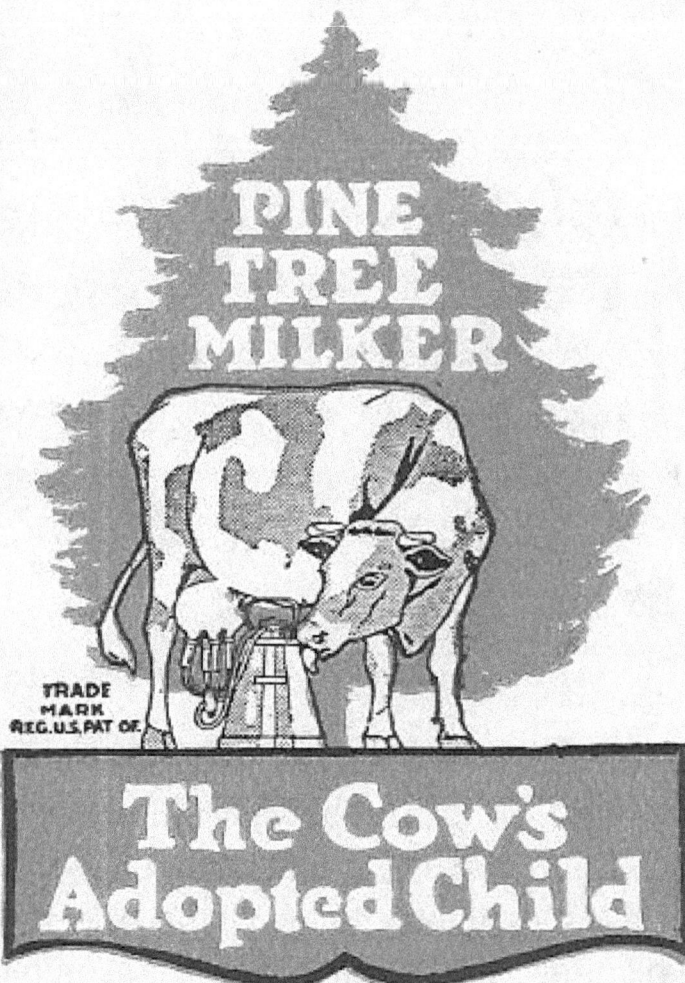

PINE TREE MILKER

TRADE MARK REG. U.S. PAT OF.

The Cow's Adopted Child

Published by the

Pine Tree Milking Machine Co.

Chicago

in the interest of Pine Tree Milker owners and other dairymen.

Pine Tree Milker
Chicago, ILL.

Pinetree 1920

PINETREE
mfg
Chicago, Ill.

The Babson Bros. (owners Of the "Pine Tree" floor milker) tried the "Surge" unit and liked the way it milked their own herd of cows. As they were very successful business men they bought it from the inventor and hired him to work for them in their research department. They ceased to market the floor unit in the early 1930's and concentrated on selling only the Pinetree "Surge" milker. That is why many early Surge milkers have a brass tag attached to them.

The Pine Tree milker at the left is in my personal milking machine collection.

PINE TREE MILKER
TRADE MARK REG. U.S. PAT. OF
The Cow's Adopted Child

"COW'S ADOPTED CHILD" MILKING WITH THE AID OF A FORD

We have always heard that you can't go into New York City's ultra society set with a Ford—but that you can go anywhere else *and get back*. We have known it to be used to run pumps and saws—but who, of our Fathers or Grandfathers, would have thought that the day would ever come when cows would be milked with an automobile?

Yet in this picture we see Mr. O. O. Groves, Pine Tree Salesman in Northwestern Wisconsin, demonstrating how simple a thing it is to milk with "The Cow's Adopted Child" and the aid of a Ford car. The cows like it better—that's why the farmers like it. "Judge It By What It Does".

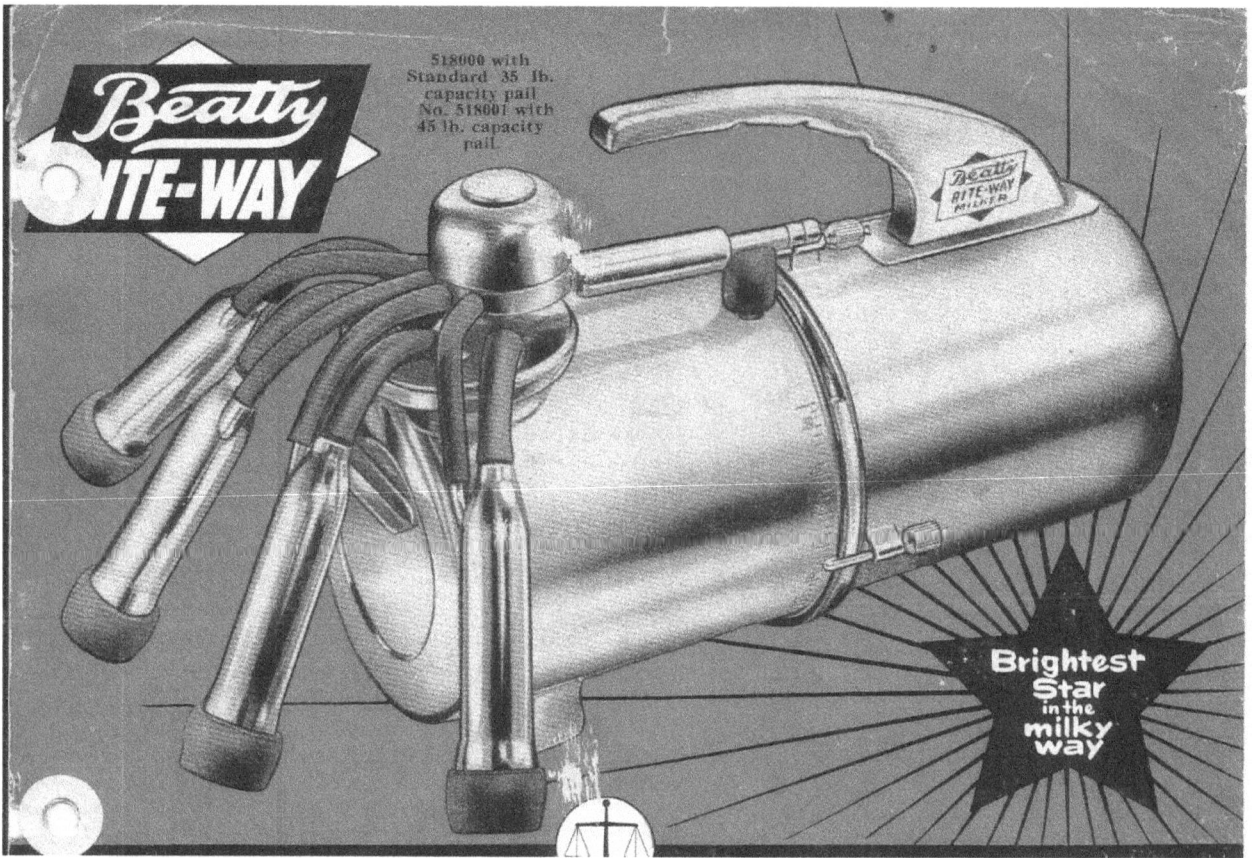

Beatty RITE-WAY

518000 with Standard 35 lb. capacity pail No. 518001 with 45 lb. capacity pail.

Beatty RITE-WAY MILKER

Brightest Star in the milky way

Rite-Way Milker
was a sub Company of the Massey-Harris Company, Limited.
Massy-Harris was established in 1847.

Sears Roebuck 1948

Rite-way Floor

This machine is brand new and has never seen milk.

Rite-way Swing

After much reading it appears that the Rite-Way Company (a sub-company of the Massey-Harris Tractor Corp.) manufactured the pulsators, claws, shells and lids for the Sears-Roebuck and Montgomery-Wards Milker. The pails for all three brands were manufactured by the Solar Company.

The Rite-Way "SWING" unit was introduced in mid-1940's as Rite-Ways answer to the "Surge" milker which seemed to be the highest selling competitor to all milking machine companies at that time. It is a two piece pail which will hold 35 lbs. of milk and splits in the middle for cleaning. It was made to be held underneath the cow by a surcingle.

Rite-Way Milker
was a sub Company of the Massey-Harris Company, Limited.
Massy-Harris was established in 1847.

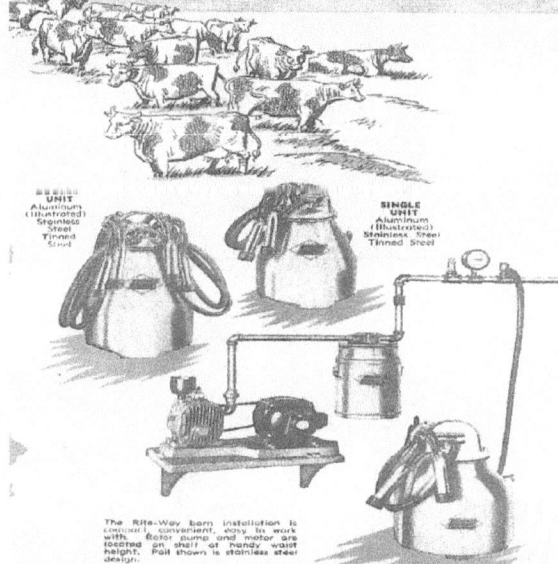

from **6 COWS TO 60**
ER *MAKES MONEY FOR YOU*

The Rite-Way barn installation is compact, convenient, easy to work with. Rotor pump and motor are located on shelf at handy waist height. Pail shown is stainless steel design.

NOW——with the aid of engineering science —the farmer with a herd of 5 or 6 cows can add extra dollars to his dairy income with machine milking equally as well as the dairyman milking 40 - 50 or 60 cows.

The new, modern Massey-Harris Rite-Way milker with its compact, scientific design, high operating efficiency and low cost performance, opens the road to money-making opportunities for dairymen large and small.

For nearly a quarter of a century the Rite-Way milker has led in the development of a higher quality milker of simple design and more dependable performance —a milker gentler in its action, easier to clean, more helpful in producing higher quality milk, low in bacteria count——and by efficient manufacturing methods to sell at the lowest possible price.

The result of this policy is that today the Massey-Harris Rite-Way milker is the fastest selling milker on the market, is used by more than 100,000 farmers, gives greater value in terms of easier milking, time-and-labor-saving, longer life and lower cost.

These features offered in the Rite-Way are particularly appreciated in busy seasons when farm help is scarce and hard to get. With the labor-saving Rite-Way, milking can be done quickly and easily without the worry of getting satisfactory help——saving the money that would otherwise be paid out in wages. On many farms where help is scarce teen-age children do the milking with a Rite-Way.

SINGLE AND DOUBLE UNIT PAILS
The Massey-Harris Rite-Way milker may be purchased with your choice of double unit or single unit vacuum-sealed pails. The double unit pail (70 lbs. capacity) milks two cows at once and is the most popular installation for faster milking and economical operation. Single unit pails (50 lbs. capacity) are available for very small herds and where it is desirable to keep daily records of individual output per cow. Both pails are available in your choice of aluminum, stainless steel or heavily tinned carbon steel. They are easy to clean, non-rusting and non-corrosive. Wide base design makes them firm seated, hard to tip.

NEW TRANSPARENT MILK TUBE

Here it is——the latest Rite-Way development——a full length milk tube you can see through. Tells at a glance when each cow is milked. Saves time and effort lost in guesswork. Just another example of the Massey-Harris Rite-Way policy of giving dairy farmers **more milker for less money.**

Rite-Way Milker
was a sub Company of the Massey-Harris Company, Limited.
Massy-Harris was established in 1847.

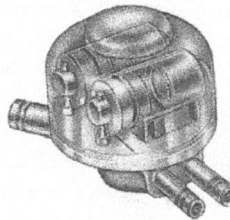

Precision-Built Pulsator Has Only Two Working Parts

Beatty Rite-Way 'Swing's' simple pulsator applies to the teats balanced suction and massage in a 4-way action. Pneumatically operated, this pulsator is superior to mechanically powered types which depend on springs, trips and gadgets. Beatty Rite-Way pulsator's suction and discharge are always uniform. Speed is adjustable by merely turning a regulating screw. The two cylinders which are the only moving parts, slide smoothly across a hardened surface; the pistons remain stationary. Design and location of air-ports gives a balanced stroke rhythm which adds to the air-cushioned suction and massage. The ease and rapidity of the pulsator's clock-like snap action is an important feature of its efficient performance.
Built with watch-like precision, the Beatty Rite-Way Pulsator can easily be taken apart and put together even with gloves on.

Rite-Way Milker
was a sub Company of the Massey-Harris Company, Limited.
Massy-Harris was established in 1847.

Beatty Rite-Way Floor Type Milker
No. 518100   Single with 50 lb. pail
No. 518101   Double with 70 lb. pail

Has all the time-proven advantages of fast, modern milking. Duplicates the calf's sucking action in suction, speed
and uniformity.

STAINLESS STEEL PAIL — Heavy gauge. Highest quality.
Large open mouth. Easy to pour with spot welded handle on
side. Easier to clean than most makes of floor type milkers.
No hidden seams. No sharp corners to harbor bacteria. Bottom
reinforced with extra metal which protects it from stable acids.
Dust-proof, dent resistant. A 70 lb. pail is supplied for double
units.

AUTOMATIC, SELF-SEALING LID — Air-tight, dust-tight.
No smoke or smudge. Vacuum milk, speeds up milking.

PULSATOR — Same easy-to-take apart filter-protected pulsator
as on the 'Swing' unit milker.

SANITARY SELF-CENTERING CLAW. Milk tube connects
underneath for self-centering of claw and even distribution of
weight on teats. Claw is made heavier to increase pull. Upward
slope of evenly spaced nipples permits maximum milk flow.
Inflations last longer as they are not bent or strained. Claw is
easy to take apart for quick thorough cleaning. Each nipple can
be brushed its full length and cleaned. Helps to produce cleaner
milk that commands higher price. Connections on claw for
fastening liners are grooved so that they will always stay on.

Beatty Rite-Way 'Swing Line' Milker
No. 518200

FOR FAST MILKING IN STANCHION BARNS OR SHEDS.
'Swing Line' milks cows from floor level directly into pipeline
which connects to 8 gal. cans. It eliminates the use of a pail.
Direct delivery saves countless hours and steps, and is more
sanitary. The milk does not have to be carried nor does it come in
contact with stable air.

ECONOMICAL TO INSTALL — 'Swing Line' permits using
part of the owner's present equipment.

SPECIFICATIONS — The 'Swing Line' milker consists of 4
teat cups, pulsator, notched handle, 2 surcingle rods the same
as used on the pail type 'Swing' milker. Weighted bar 11¾ lbs.
and approximately 92 in. of flexible rubber suction hose and 97
in. of transparent hose are included. The plastic hose is the same
type of hose as used on the Floor Type Milker.

Weighted bar of chrome plated rust-resisting steel holds
down the teat cups. Prevents them from creeping. Applies
a steady weight for fast milking.

EASILY ADJUSTABLE — Like the 'Swing' unit milker, 'Swing
Line' can be adjusted for teat cup positioning by simply changing
the hanging position of the milker or adjusting the position of
the surcingle.

EASY TO TAKE APART AND CLEAN — The 'Swing Line'
milker is simplicity itself. Teat cups and pulsator are simple to
take apart and to thoroughly clean.

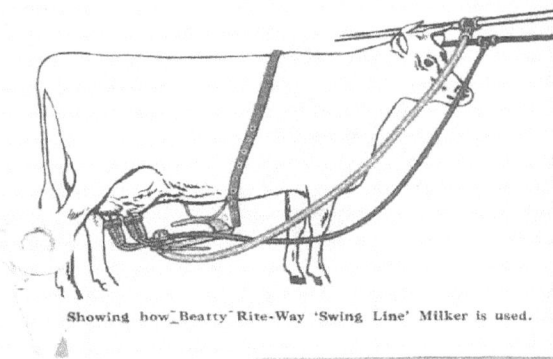

Beatty
Rite-Way
'Floor Type'
Milker

TRANSPARENT PLASTIC HOSE — Shows the amount of
milk flow and indicates when milking is finished. Safeguards
health of cow. Speeds up milking. Hose is 7 times stronger than
rubber. Scientifically treated to resist cold and heat.

Beatty Rite-Way 'Swing Line' Milker Unit

Showing how Beatty Rite-Way 'Swing Line' Milker is used.

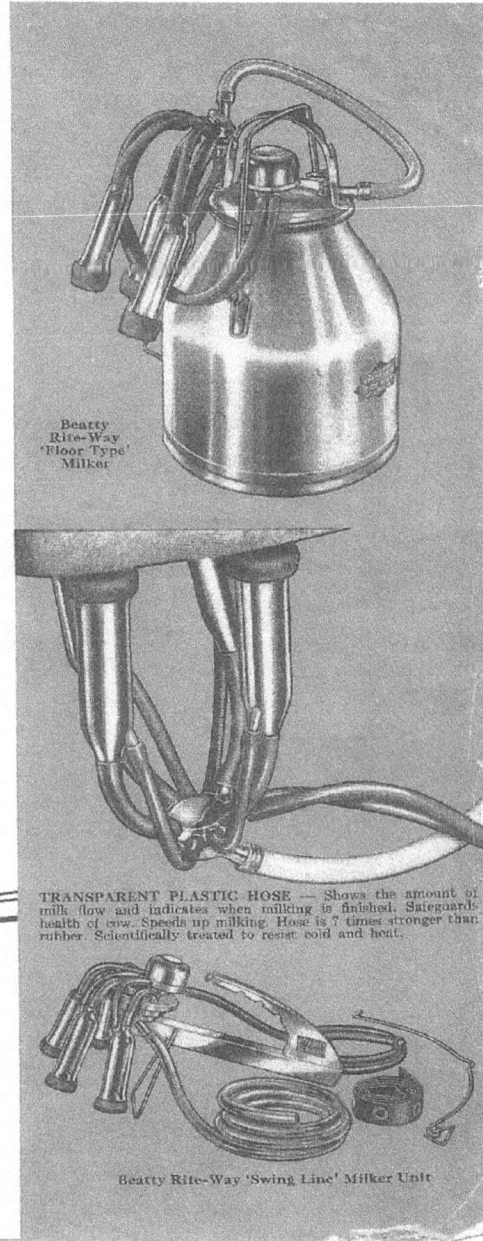

The
SHARPLES
MECHANICAL
MILKER

SOLD AND GUARANTEED BY

The Sharples Separator Co.

The Sharples Mechanical Milker

Guaranteed by the
Sharples Separator Co.
West Chester Pa.

Sharples
West Chester, PA
earliest patent 1903

THE SHARPLES
MECHANICAL MILKER

HAS THE TEAT CUP WITH
THE   UPWARD   SQUEEZE

Dairy Specialty Company,

Sole Manufacturers

WEST CHESTER, PENNSYLVANIA, U. S. A.

Graphics are from Mike Gleason collection of milker manuals and advertising brochures

The Great Features

T IS a long and difficult road that the Sharples inventors and mechanics have followed unceasingly for the past ten years in their determination to produce a perfect mechanical milker. Starting with an intimate and expert knowledge of dairy needs and cow conditions, gained through their life-time connection with dairy methods and machinery of the highest class, and backed by unlimited capital, unequaled facilities, and a complete knowledge of all previous work done in this line, they nevertheless found the task a difficult one and yet the completed, perfected milker is marvelously simple, convenient and durable.

All great inventions have gone through the complicated and inefficient stage to the simple and effective, and nearly always it seems strange that the perfected device was not the first one thought of. So it is with the Sharples Mechanical Milker.

"TEAT-CUP WITH THE UPWARD SQUEEZE"

During the long time spent in perfecting the apparatus, we have invented and incorporated a number of most important features, never before applied in connection with a mechanical milker and these inventions, which can be used in no other milking machine, being covered by broad and comprehensive patents secured in the principal dairy countries of the world, are the basis of the success and perfection of the work of our milker. Most important of these new inventions is the " *Teat-Cup with the Upward Squeeze.*" Without the use of this vital principle we firmly believe that no milking machine can be successful, while its use fully overcomes the one greatest barrier that has stood in the way of a perfect milking machine.

The simple and easily understood principle of this most necessary feature, is this:—after the drawing of each squirt or stream of milk from the teat, the tissue and blood within the teat shall be gently massaged or pressed backwards toward the udder.

The failure to do this invariably results in congested teats and sooner or later in injury to the cow, the extent of this depending on her hardiness. But by the proper use of this all-important principle made possible in the Sharples Mechanical Milker, the teats and udder of either the most delicate or the most hardy cow are alike kept in a soft, cool, natural and perfect condition.

A pulsating and variable suction, applied to the teat, has long been tried. We, ourselves, used it for some years in our experiments, but never in a single instance did it prove a perfect or successful mechanism for the purpose of milking.

Such intermittent suction but partially relieves the teat for a moment and has no effect in returning the tissues pulled down by the full suction of the previous moment, and when this suction or downward working is applied again and again at each pulsation, the teat becomes congested, hard and feverish, inevitably resulting in course of time, in injury to the cow. Moreover, in addition to the injury to the cow resulting from the constant pulsating suction, there is the serious difficulty that the milk can neither be quickly nor thoroughly drawn. The tissue and blood drawn down and congested at the lower end of the teat, swell and harden the teat at that point, thus partially closing the milk outlet and seriously interfering with the milk flow.

A *complete* relief from suction or downward pull, followed by a gentle massage or upward squeeze, at each pulsation or drawing of a squirt of milk, is what is needed and is what is imperatively necessary, and that is what the Sharples Mechanical Milker does, it being constructed under our broad patents covering this method. This is the crucial point of any successful mechanical milker, and until we invented the method we never dared offer a milker to dairymen, though long before that time we were owners of patents on the best pulsating suction milkers ever devised.

Graphics are from Mike Gleason collection of milker manuals and advertising brochures

Sharples
West Chester, PA
earliest patent 1903

Sharples

SHARPLES
mfg. West Chester, Pa
1914

Sharples Milker purchased at Anderson Farm auction in Preble, NY in mid 1980's

Pulsator came from Riehlman Bros. Farm in Homer, NY in mid-1980's Pulsator weighs about 10 pounds.

Milker and Pulsator are from Mike Gleason collection of Milking Machines

Sharples
West Chester, PA
earliest patent 1903

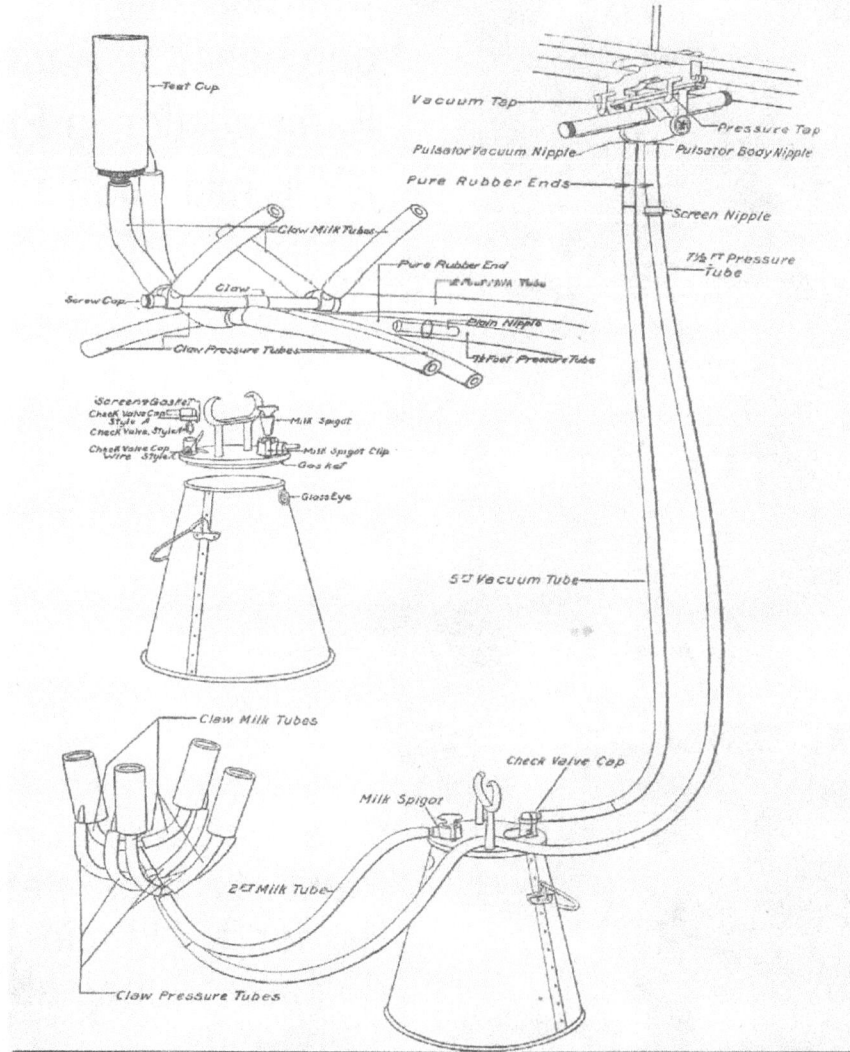

Graphics are from Mike Gleason collection of milker manuals and advertising brochures

Sharples
West Chester, PA
earliest patent 1903

Sharples

After work one day in the mid -1980's I stopped at the diner in town to have a cup of coffee, "One of my life's habits at that time". I sat down with a couple of old farmers who were there. In the conversation I asked them if they had any old "milker" parts still around their farms? They laughed at me when I told them I was collecting old "milking machines." One of the gentlemen told me of a machine called the "Sharples" that he had milked with when he was a young man doing relief milking for a neighbor. A bit of time went by and the farmer this man had milked for in years past was having a full liquidation sale as one of the owners was retiring. At that sale I managed to purchase a 1910 Sharples pail and lid.

A couple of weeks went by and working for another farmer I was telling him about my purchases at the auction. He lived a couple of miles from the where the auction was held. He also told me that the "Sharples" was the first mechanical milker that his father ever bought. There may even be some old "Sharples" parts in the attic above the old shop. He checked, and there were! He gave them to me.

In that gift were the pulsator, 4 milker shells, and a milker claw for the "Sharples" milking machine. If you are lucky enough, it will appear.

Graphics are from Mike Gleason collection of milking machines in Herkimer, NY

Simplicity Milker
Patented August 16, 1910 by Floyd B. Groff
St. Johnsville,

Only 2 of
the
Simplicity
Milkers
are known
to exist.
They are
owned by
a couple
of
nephews
of the
inventor
living in
St.
Johnsville,
NY. The
side
picture
was taken
by Mike
Gleason

**Floyd B. Groff's
Patent
Simplicity Milker**

**Nature's Method of Milking
Imitated**

THE SIMPLICITY MILKER was patented August 16, 1910, but prior to that time was successfully used on the farm of Fayette Groff, in the town of St. Johnsville, Montgomery County, N. Y.

The teat-cup is of metal and the only rubber used is the rubber apron in the mouth of each teat-cup. This is held in place by a clasp and can easily be removed and cleaned. A metal connector connects the teat-cup with the tube running to the pail. At the base of each teat-cup is an inspection glass which at once shows whether or not the milk flows. The teat-cup and part which contains the inspection glass operates by means of a ball and socket joint, permitting the teat-cup to be adjusted to any position. Along the outside of each teat-cup is an air tube, which, when the milker is in operation, causes suction to take place upon the upper part of the teat and lower part of the cow's udder

The milker proper and which rests on the pail is entirely of metal and consists of only four part, viz: The head, two buckets, and an axle or pivot upon which the cups balance. Each cup acts independently of the other and its operation is regulated by the flow of the milk.

Any power may be used to operate this milker. The power acting upon this device causes the milk to flow from the teats of one cow, until the bucket is filled on one side, when it drops automatically and

flows into the pail. This continues alternately until the udder of the cow is relieved from milk. It will be observed that the relief offered to the cow's udder is entirely controlled by the flow of milk and this device accommodates itself equally well to a hard milking cow and to an easy milking cow. By this device there is no constant draw upon the teat of the cow and no injurious effect results either to the teat or udder of the cow.

The operation of this milker is almost an exact imitation of what occurs when the

calf sucks the cow. The rubber in the mouth of the teat-cup represents the tongue of the calf. The milk flowing from the teat into the bucket represents the milk flowing into the mouth of the calf. The bucket emptying into the pail represents the swallowing of the milk by the calf. By this milking device when the bucket empties into the pail, the suction is relieved almost in the same manner as the suction is relieved when the calf swallows the milk.

By the operation of this milker two cows are milked at the same time, the milk from one cow flowing into one bucket of the milker and the milk from the other cow flowing into the other.

This milker is simple in construction. The parts are durable. It is easy to keep clean and to operate. Anyone who observes this milker in operation will at once see that the question of mechanical milking has been solved.

The Surge Milker

PINE TREE MILKING MACHINE CO.
2843 WEST 19TH ST. CHICAGO

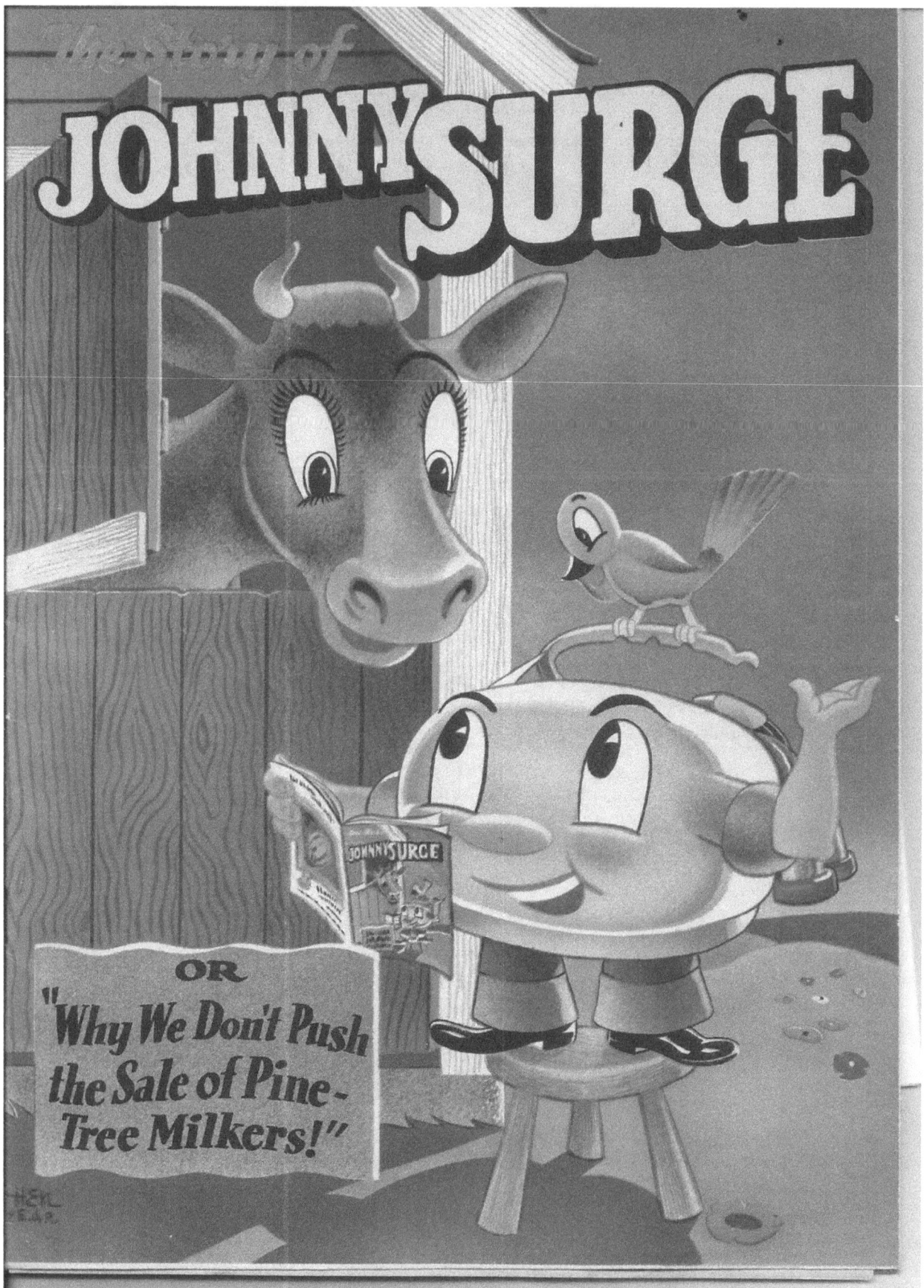

The Story of
JOHNNY SURGE

OR
"Why We Don't Push
the Sale of Pine-
Tree Milkers!"

Surge Milker
First marketed as the "Pine Tree Surge Milker" around 1922 or 23 by the
Pine Tree Milker Co.
2843 West 19th St., Chicago, ILL.

The above information is from a 1930's "Surge Milker Advertising booklet in
the Mike Gleason, Herkimer NY reference collection

Surge Milker
First marketed as the "Pine Tree Surge Milker" around 1922 or 23 by the Pine Tree Milker Co.
2843 West 19th St., Chicago, ILL.

"THE MILLION DOLLAR PINE TREE MILKER"

It was into this relatively unexplored and possibly hostile setting that Babson Bros. entered the milking machine field with what was called the *"Pine Tree Milking Machine,"* named after the *"Four Pine Farm"* which was owned by Mr. F. K. Babson. The milker was invented by A. C. Macartney. *"More than $1,000,000.00 stood back of the inventor at every step,"* reads the Old Pine Tree literature. A laboratory constructed on the Four Pine Farm supplied a fully equipped machine shop headed by *America's foremost milking machine expert.*

The Pine Tree Milker brought about several innovations, but it still followed the then standard floor pail with a claw-type, double-action teat cup assembly. The simple, detachable *pulsator* of the Pine Tree was one of its new features, plus the fact that the milker carried an *extraordinary three year guarantee.* It was superbly built and well-engineered and rapidly gained considerable sales acceptance.

Until 1910, Babson Bros. had been best known as an installment or time payment mail order house specializing in items such as the Edison Phonograph, Men's Made-To-Order Clothing, Burlington Watches, The Olde Tan Harness, and many other items. This type of marketing was just beginning to change the buying habits of Americans by allowing customers the savings of buying direct from a distributor with such advantages as *Free Trial* and *Twelve Months to Pay.*

Shortly prior to 1910, the Company began to place more emphasis on dairy farm equipment, and it was about this time

7-a. *Test milking the Pine Tree Milker.*
7-b. *The 1917 Pine Tree Milker—Babson's first milker.*

Above information was sent to me by
Rex Sprietsma
Manager, Electronic Marketing
and Market Analisis
Westfalis-Surge, Inc

Surge Milker
First marketed as the "Pine Tree Surge Milker" around 1922 or 23 by the
Pine Tree Milker Co.
2843 West 19th St., Chicago, ILL.

THE BIRTH OF THE SURGE

One fall day in 1922, there appeared in Babson's Chicago office a farm boy engineer by the name of Herbert McCornack. McCornack had contacted several milking machine companies with his *new idea in cow milking*, but received scant attention. A relative who was then selling Pine Tree Machines brought him to Chicago and introduced him to the three Babson brothers.

Herbert McCornack began talking about the strangulation of the cow's udder by the milking machines in use at that time. He went on to pull out of a box the first Surge Milker ever built. Crude as it was, the suspended pail and other safety features were there. These fast milking and safety features were to become famous around the world in the years that followed.

McCornack pointed to the short tubes which took the milk from the cow to the bucket, and emphasized this as a solution to many of the sanitation problems of floor-type machines. He also stressed the lively milking action created by the one-point suspension of the bucket, hung by means of a strap or *Surcingle* as it eventually came to be called. This *surging* action permitted a tug-and-pull movement of the milker during normal milking, similar to the tugging and pulling of a calf.

Herbert McCornack made claims that the machine had a *surging* action that made it milk faster and therefore get more milk, that it was easy to produce cleaner milk, and that it would *cut down on garget*. Those claims needed proving to the Babson brothers, and they set about doing it in 1923.

9-a. "THE SURGE"—in 1924 . . . the new look in milking machines.

le://C:\WINDOWS\TEMP\SURGEisBorn2.jpg

**Above information was sent to me by
Rex Sprietsma
Manager, Electronic Marketing
and Market Analisis
Westfalis-Surge, Inc**

107

Surge Milker
First marketed as the "Pine Tree Surge Milker" around 1922 or 23 by the
Pine Tree Milker Co.
2843 West 19th St., Chicago, ILL.

The Surge Milker
Pine Tree Milking Machine Co.

10/15/01

Above information was sent to me by
Rex Sprietsma
Manager, Electronic Marketing
and Market Analisis
Westfalis-Surge, Inc

Surge Milker
First marketed as the "Pine Tree Surge Milker" around 1922 or 23 by the
Pine Tree Milker Co.
2843 West 19th St., Chicago, ILL.

A number of hand-made machines under the label of Pine
Tree "Surge" were installed on certain farms for experimental
Work under the direction of the New York Experiment Station
At Geneva. A bacteriologist was hired to check and record the
Quality of the milk taken. It wasn't long before everyone in-
Volved in the test Knew that this new kind of milker,not only
Milked cows better, but substantially reduced the bacteria
Count.

What came of the first production line was a milking
Machine that had several additional features as well as its
Surging action, which gave it its name. A smooth easy to clean,
Spun-steel pail . . . the first truly pneumatic pulsator mounted
Only a few inches from the udder. . . the first one-piece inflation and shell assembly which could be taken apart in a matter
of seconds . . . and the first shut-off nipples which allowed
the dropping of teat cups on milked out quarters. . .were
some of the features that made the SURGE milker a great milking machine from the very beginning

The original Surge Milker met with unusual success despite
Some ridicule of its suspension feature. Many things con-
tributed to the success of the Surge. In addition to the unique
design which allowed its fast milking and tug-and-pull action,
there was also its easy-to-clean short tube feature. The free
trial method of selling, the training the user received in proper
milking, the installation and regular servicing of Surge machines. . . all thes became part of the Surge success story.

10-a An early Ad stressing the "Surging Action"of the
milker

10-b Advertising painting of the 1936 Stainless Steel Surge
milker

10-c Surge milker in use in one Certified Dairy
in Indiana.

**Above information was sent to me by
Rex Sprietsma
Manager, Electronic Marketing
and Market Analisis
Westfalis-Surge, Inc**

Surge Milker
First marketed as the "Pine Tree Surge Milker" around 1922 or 23 by the
Pine Tree Milker Co.
2843 West 19th St., Chicago, ILL.

THE SURGE MILKER

The Surge Milker Is Entirely Different Because—

It has no long milk tubes and it has no milk claws. Pick out twenty or thirty different makes of milking machines and put them in a row— no two are exactly alike. One has this feature and one has that; but they *are* all alike in that everyone of them, without exception, has long milk tubes and each has a milk claw. So—for convenience, we call them Claw Type Machines. The Surge has no long tubes. It has no claws. That fact at once divides mechanical milkers into two classes—the Surge Milker in one group—and all other milking machines in the other.

Long tubes are hard to clean—a fact that no amount of talk can change. Milk claws are bacteria catchers—ask any milk inspector. The Surge has *neither*, while all claw type machines have *both*. All other milkers are claw type machines and are consequently hard to clean.

We feel entirely justified in speaking thus frankly because we, ourselves, make a claw type machine. We have made one for ten years—the tried and proved Pine Tree Milker and we are proud of it, proud of its record of success. To the man who can be satisfied with *any* kind of claw type milker at all, we recommend our machine—we ask you to compare it, point by point with any competing milking machine at any price whatever. It is a thoroughly good milking machine brought as nearly up to date as *any* claw type milker can be brought *but* it can't compete with the Surge!

It isn't because we have nothing else to offer that we urge you to install a Surge Milker rather than any kind of claw type machine—not at all. Ten years' experience with claw type machines enables us to recognize their limitations.

Just as the Surge made our own machine out of date overnight, just so it made *all* claw type milking machines old fashioned. It can have no real competition because there is nothing else like it—nothing with which to compare it. That it must be easy to clean is at once apparent. That it will milk cows better can easily be shown. One big reason that the Surge milks quicker and cleaner is

Because—

A claw type milker

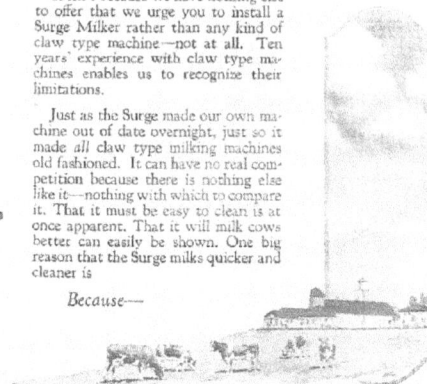

The above information is from a 1930's "Surge Milker Advertising booklet in the Mike Gleason, Herkimer NY reference collection

Surge Milker
First marketed as the "Pine Tree Surge Milker" around 1922 or 23 by the
Pine Tree Milker Co.
2843 West 19th St., Chicago, ILL.

"JUST COWS"—H. E. Swartz, Richfield Springs, New
York, "A cross of nearly every breed"

From Willard J. Hall, Manager of Kingsford
Farms near Oswego, New York—see Surge installation here shown on page 19. Mr. Hall tells
how well The Surge has served them in this letter:

"The Surge Milker, which you installed about a year ago
enables us to milk 26 to 34 cows in about an hour with two
men operating three units. Before it took four men one and a
half hours to do this.

We are making much cleaner milk than we did by hand. No
trouble producing low bacteria count milk. No udder trouble.
The fact that there are no long tubes or claws influenced me
most in buying the Surge. It's very easy to keep clean.

Outside of operating expense, the maintaining expense has
been $15.00 or less than 1½c per day on each Surge Unit. It
is a pleasure to recommend The Surge Milker."

BROWN SWISS—W. E. Jones Estate, Charlotte, New
York, Walter E. Jones, Manager

The above information is from a 1930's "Surge Milker Advertising booklet in
the Mike Gleason, Herkimer NY reference collection

Surge Milker
First marketed as the "Pine Tree Surge Milker" around 1922 or 23 by the Pine Tree Milker Co.
2843 West 19th St., Chicago, ILL.

PINE TREE MILKING MACHINE CO.

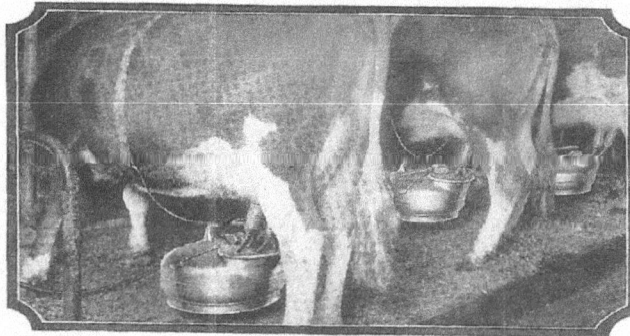

The Surge Milker at home—Four Pine Farm

Four Pine Guernseys

Four Pine Farm is perhaps best known as the home of King of Chilmark 20798, one of the greatest Guernsey sires of all time. When he died at the age of 16, he was buried on Four Pine Lawn.

King was the sire of 37 A. R. daughters, eight making records of over 700 lbs. of butter fat. Cows now on test will almost certainly bring the number of his A. R. daughters to 40 and there is a good chance that enough of his daughters will pass 700 lbs. to enable him to equal the record of any Guernsey bull living or dead.

Contrafuria No. 29090, in her 11th year, made a record of 15,765 lbs. of milk, 745 lbs. butter fat in Class AA—7th at the time and her third A. R. record.

A half sister Lilyett No. 33416, made 703 lbs. of fat in her 11th year. Two of her daughters made state records.

During the last ten years more than 50 A. R. records have been made at Four Pine, more state records have been made than in any other Guernsey herd in Illinois and several of these were national records. Since 1918 test cows have been milked with the Pine Tree Milker and since 1923 with the Surge Milker.

Cows are now on test whose mothers, grandmothers and great grandmothers were machine milked. Their records and the condition of their udders are the best advertisement we can write.

Perfected on the Farm

Four Pine Farm near Hinsdale, Illinois, is the real home of The Surge Milker. Our first milker was developed at Four Pine ten years ago and given the name Pine Tree. The Surge milked a herd of Pure Bred Guernseys, through an entire lactation period before a unit was sold. In addition to the regular herd, we bought a bunch of freak cows of all breeds and no breed. Wherever any of our men found a peculiarly hard milker or uneven udder, the animal was bought and shipped to Four Pine and The Surge was given the job of getting the milk. It got it, too. All that happened three years ago and since that time, the use of The Surge has spread to all states and all breeds. It is no longer new but is a thoroughly proved machine.

We have never sold an experiment. Every new article, even every little change gets a good long trial at Four Pine before it is offered for sale. We build milkers in our factory but before we build anything we get the opinion of the cows in the Four Pine herd. And that means something — as you will soon see.

21

The above information is from a 1930's "Surge Milker Advertising booklet in the Mike Gleason, Herkimer NY reference collection

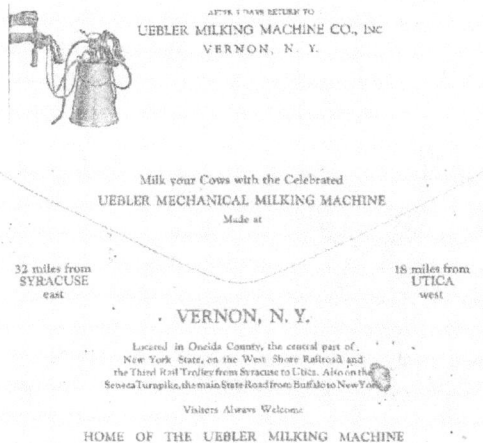

AFTER 5 DAYS RETURN TO
UEBLER MILKING MACHINE CO., INC
VERNON, N. Y.

Milk your Cows with the Celebrated
UEBLER MECHANICAL MILKING MACHINE
Made at

32 miles from
SYRACUSE
east

18 miles from
UTICA
west

· VERNON, N. Y.

Located in Oneida County, the central part of
New York State, on the West Shore Railroad and
the Third Rail Trolley from Syracuse to Utica. Also on the
Seneca Turnpike, the main State Road from Buffalo to New York

Visitors Always Welcome

HOME OF THE UEBLER MILKING MACHINE

Uebler oldest

The milking machines
above are in my collection
in Herkimer, NY

Uebler Milker

One Saturday in early November 2007 I decided to take a trip to a friend's home in Morrisville, NY. After a couple hours of drinking coffee, I decided to visit a couple of milking machine dealers in the area. Neither dealer had anything I could use (old parts), but both had me leave my card and promised to call me if anything surfaced. I shrugged Okay to an average day collecting and went home. In the meantime when I got home, a piece I had placed a bid on had finished selling on Ebay, and I didn't get it. I was bummed. Two misses in one week. That's the way collecting goes sometimes. Five days later one of the dealers called and said that he had a lead for me. He asked me if I had I ever heard of the **Uebler** Milker? Well. I wasn't long in calling and finding out the "scoop." I found there was a retired dairyman's wife who had three Uebler Milkers for sale, and she lived in the town of Holland Patent, NY. He gave me her phone number and I called her right away. These units were her father's, which he had bought in 1940. She and her husband milked with them from 1947 until 1958 when they sold the cows. I made arrangements to meet her the next morning to look at them.

My wife and I headed out the next morning on a 60 mile road trip to Holland Patent. We drove into a neat farmstead and a lady came from the house to greet us. I introduced myself and Janet and started to look over the building and talk about their farming experience. About an hour later she took us to the milk house to see the elusive "Uebler" milking machine. Once I spied the milking machines, I knew that I was not leaving without buying all three. They were in near-perfect condition and still had the rubber pieces from the last time they milked a cow. The elusive "Uebler was found and in it's new home. The next journey is to find the owner's manual for this beast.

A road trip to find an owner's manual for "**Uebler**" Milking machines was on 11-26-07. The day began at 5:30 AM. With my first cup of coffee in hand, I went to the diner in Lafayette for breakfast and general bull shoot and was home by 7:30 AM. I went to the computer to find the address for Eastern Crown Inc., located in Vernon NY so that I could mapquest directions. I left home about 8:30 AM. After about an hour of travel I stopped at a Nice & Easy "stop and rob." After getting gas and another cup of coffee to go, I asked a couple of older gentlemen for final directions to my destination. As it turned out, I was only about 6 miles and two turns from where I wanted to be. I arrived at E.C.I. about 10:15. In talking with the parts man, I got the distinct feeling that he thought I had a screw loose

for collecting old milking machines. I bought 2 sets of inflations for the "**Empire**" milking machine from late 1930's. And the parts man gave me another place I should stop and check for milking machine parts (an older established farm machinery dealership). This part of the trip found me backtracking about 15 miles to town of Munnsville, NY The owner of this dealership didn't have any manuals or parts on hand that he knew about, but he told me that his father had died a couple of months ago and that he had yet to go through his dad's basement which was full of old paper stuff from over the years. (Apparently his father had a hard time parting with old advertising pieces also.) He said if he found anything relating to old milking machines he would give me a call. After getting lost a couple more times I arrived home about 3:00 PM. A lot of road's traveled; no new milkers or manuals were found, but many nice people were met and hopefully some new pieces will be coming down the road in time. I left many "Mike's Milker" cards throughout Central NY.

UNIVERSAL MILKING MACHINE

THE UNIVERSAL MILKING MACHINE CO.
COLUMBUS, OHIO

The Universal has Won its Way

THAT you may see why the Universal Milking Machine has gained steadily in public favor, why it is today recognized as the leader, why it is in use where other machines have failed, and why you should use it yourself, is the object of this little book.

In it we have not tried to tell you anything more than the actual facts as borne out by the experience of many users. Much more could be said of exceptional cases, but it is the intention to show what can be done in the average dairy by the use of this machine.

The Universal Milking Machine was not launched with a great amount of capital for exploitation. It has had to win its way on merit exclusively, and the character of its users is proof that it has won its favor among practical men who have been able to secure with it practical results.

As perfect mechanically as we can make it, the success of the machine depends upon the user. Its practicability and its economy have been demonstrated so often that they are no longer open to question. The man who uses the Universal Milking Machine correctly will find it a labor saver, reliable, safe, convenient and effective.

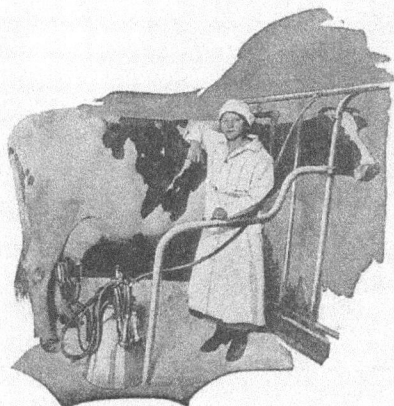

THE UNIVERSAL MILKING
MACHINE COMPANY
Columbus, Ohio

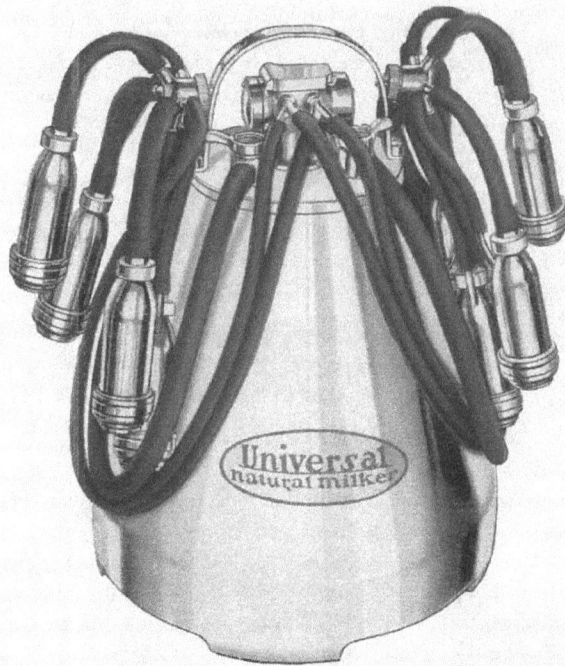

The Universal Milking Machine Co.
Waukesha, Wisconsin
Started sales around 1925

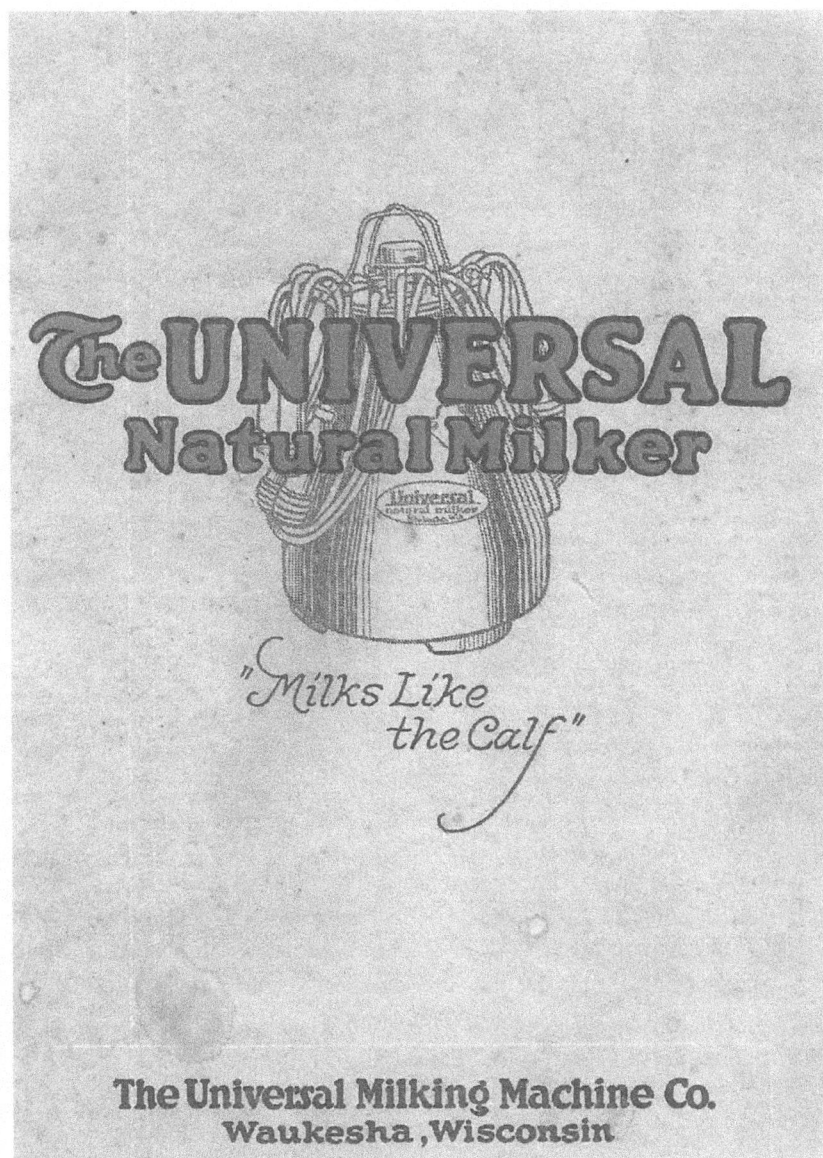

The UNIVERSAL
Natural Milker

"Milks Like
the Calf"

The Universal Milking Machine Co.
Waukesha, Wisconsin

This page is from Mike Gleason, Herkimer, NY collection manuals and reference materials

The Universal Milking Machine Co.
Waukesha, Wisconsin
Started sales around 1925

The History of Milking Machines

EVER since dairying became a separate, recognized industry, men of inventive minds have been constantly trying to figure out how to simplify the job of milking—to make it an easy mechanical operation instead of a hard, tiresome, time-consuming hand chore.

The milking machine is commonly thought of as one of the newer inventions of the age like the automobile, radio, and other modern scientific developments. As a matter of fact, however, milking machine history dates back farther than even such long-accepted public utilities as the telephone, telegraph, and railway transportation. Men were thinking about milkng machines as far back as 1819. But nothing of a really practical nature was accomplished until 1878, at which time work in this direction began in earnest, leading to the development of the milking machine to its present state of perfection.

Milking Tubes

The first "milking machine" consisted of tubes that were inserted in the cow's teats and pushed up the "milk cistern" in the udder. The idea was that the milk would drain out by gravity. But like many other "bright" ideas, this one didn't work out as well in practice as it did in theory. In the first place, it was no easy job to perform this operation on even a good-natured cow twice a day—it was just about as easy to do the job by hand, the old fashioned way. In the second place, it was hard on the cow—and bad for her. If the tubes were not carefully sterilized before being pushed into the teat, they were liable to cause a dangerous infection. And frequent insertion of the tubes into the teats and udder would set up an irritation that caused the cow a lot of discomfort and made her hold her milk.

No less than five different makes of these "milk draining" devices were put on the market between 1878 and 1896. The basic idea—mechanical milking—was all right, but the method was all wrong, so these first milking machines never became very popular.

In developing milking machines, the beginning was naturally very crude, the same as in developing any new machine. There is just as great a difference between the milking machine of 1896 and the present-day perfected UNIVERSAL NATURAL MILKER, as there is between Cyrus McCormick's first reaper, made in 1831, and the wonderfully efficient self-binder of today.

Pressure Machines or "Lactators"

While some men were trying to work out the milking tube theory to a point where it would be practical (a goal that was never reached) others were working along entirely different lines, developing pressure machines, also known as "lactators." Twenty-five of these were produced between 1878 and 1895. The principle of the pressure machine was to apply pressure to the base of the teat, next to the udder, in this way closing the milk channel of the teat and by applying continuous downward pressure, forcing the milk out. Hand milking, however, is an example of the only really successful application of this principle in milking.

Vacuum or Suction Type Milkers

The first vacuum or "suction type" milker was made in Newark, N. J., in 1878 and during the next twenty-eight years, or until 1906, approximately fifty different milkers of this type were produced. Of this number, only one make proved good enough to win recognition that kept it from passing out of existence along with the others.

Lots of Milkers—But Not Many Practical Ones

The annual reports of the U. S. Patent Commissioner show that during the period of 1872 to 1901, inclusive, there were some 89 milking machine patents granted to over 70 different inventors, showing that a great deal of study and inventive genius had been directed toward the solution of the problem of mechanical milking. But none of these machines fulfilled the requirements of the farmer and dairyman, so new ones continued to be produced and they in turn gave way to still more advanced developments.

UNIVERSAL NATURAL MILKER [2]

The Universal Milking Machine Co.
Waukesha, Wisconsin
Started sales around 1925

The ten years between 1906 and 1916 witnessed greater progress in the advancement of milking machines than all the time that had gone before. And yet, most of these new machines, about fifty in number, fell short of the successful milker in some respect.

Real success was not in sight until the principle of SUCTION was applied to milking machines—a comparatively recent development. As previously stated, the first principle to be applied to mechanical milking was that of drawing the milk from the cow's udder by means of inserting tubes and allowing the milk to flow out by gravity. The second method was that of squeezing or pressing the milk from the udder. The third and only practical method is that of suction, which is the principle used today in all successful milking machines, and is the only method that has ever been found that will successfully milk a cow. No machine squeezes the milk from the teat. The squeeze of the rubber liner in the teat cup is for the purpose of massaging the teat. For more detailed information regarding the squeeze in cups, see page 14.

Of the various machines on the market we find still another division or classification of types—"push rod" and "pipe line." Nearly all the former use what is known as the non-inflation type teat cup, while most pipe line machines use the inflation type of teat cup.

Requirements of Perfect Milking Machines

The true principle desired in a mechanical milker is the exact duplication of the action of the calf's mouth on the teat. The calf while sucking applies vacuum or suction to the teat at intervals. These intervals are known as pulsations. The intervals produced by the calf are due to the fact that a calf is obliged to take its breath and swallow, which relieves the teat of the suction at that moment, and allows the blood in the teat, which has been retarded by suction, to flow back. In swallowing, the calf's tongue is forced against the roof of the mouth, which exerts pressure on the teat FROM THE END FIRST, TOWARD THE UDDER, further assisting in the return of the blood in the teat by massaging. These pulsations and the massaging action of the calf's tongue are exactly reproduced by the Universal pulsator and inflation type teat cup.

The calf, after all, is the ORIGINAL NATURAL MILKER, and the Universal so completely duplicates the action of the calf's mouth on the teat that it has truly and rightfully earned the name UNIVERSAL NATURAL MILKER. It employs sound principles that assure permanent success.

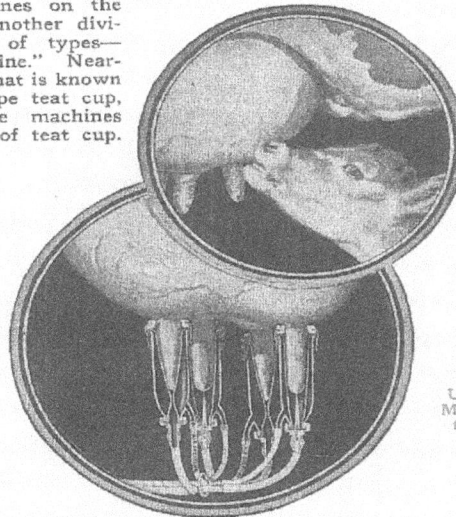

The Universal Milks Like the Calf

[3]   MILKS LIKE THE CALF

This page is from Mike Gleason, Herkimer, NY collection manuals and referance materials

The Universal Milking Machine Co.
Waukesha, Wisconsin
Started sales around 1925

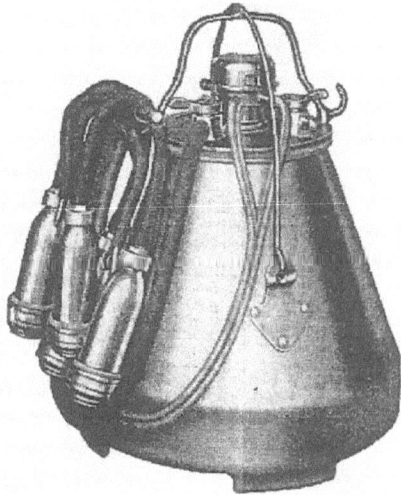

Single Unit Milker

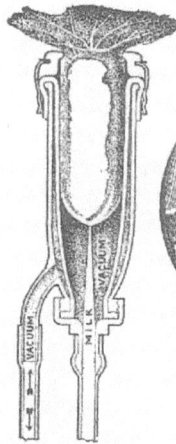

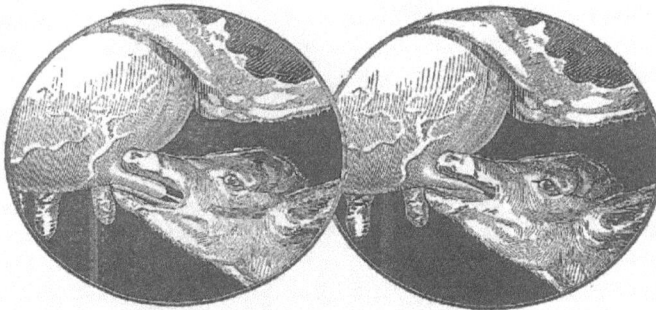

MILKING   MASSAGING

The Universal Natural Milker
Milks Like the Calf

MILKING

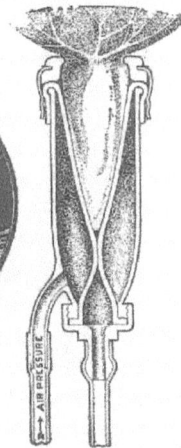

MASSAGING

This page is from Mike Gleason, Herkimer, NY collection manuals and referance materials

The Universal Milking Machine Co.
Waukesha, Wisconsin
Started sales around 1925

THE IMPROVED, TYPE F

Universal natural milker

WITH DIAPHRAM CONTROL PULSATOR
AND
QUAD-O-MATIC SPEED REGULATOR

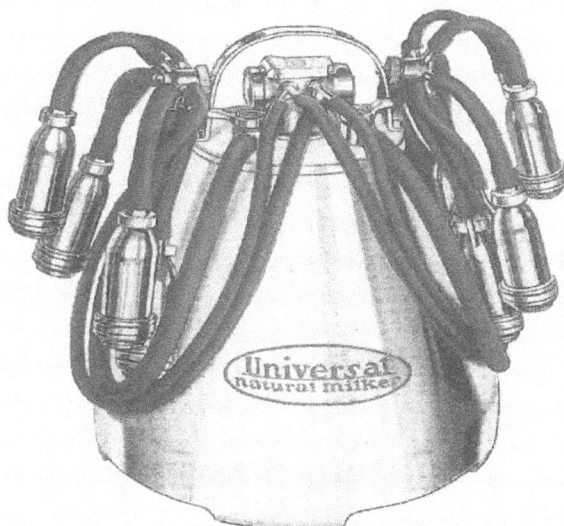

"MILKS LIKE THE CALF"
AND
"ALTERNATES LIKE MILKING WITH HANDS"

UNIVERSAL MILKING MACHINE CO.

FACTORY AND GENERAL OFFICES	EASTERN FACTORY BRANCH
WAUKESHA, WIS.	SYRACUSE, N. Y.

This page is from Mike Gleason, Herkimer, NY collection manuals and referance materials

The Universal Milking Machine Co.
Waukesha, Wisconsin
Started sales around 1925

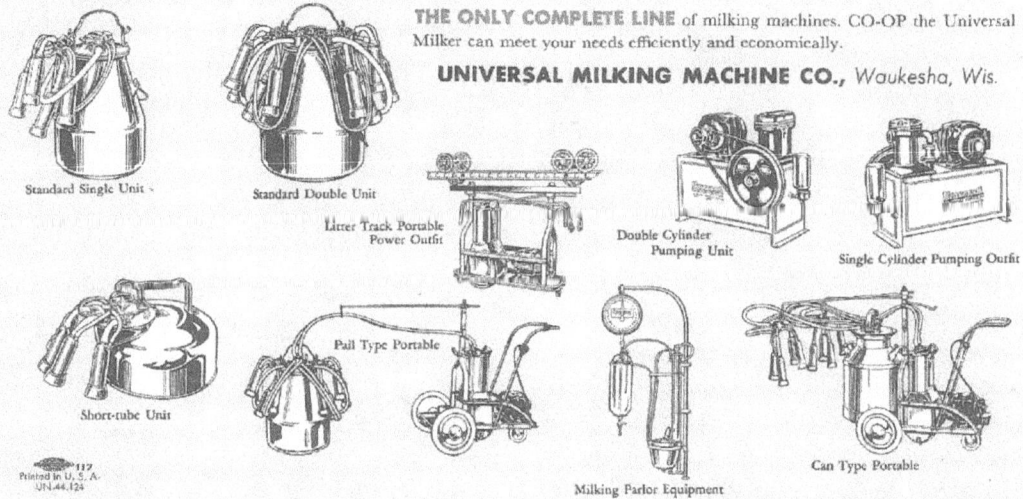

THE ONLY COMPLETE LINE of milking machines. CO-OP the Universal Milker can meet your needs efficiently and economically.

UNIVERSAL MILKING MACHINE CO., Waukesha, Wis.

Standard Single Unit

Standard Double Unit

Litter Track Portable Power Outfit

Double Cylinder Pumping Unit

Single Cylinder Pumping Outfit

Short-tube Unit

Pail Type Portable

Milking Parlor Equipment

Can Type Portable

I am in total awe of the human ability to see a need and to fill that void. The graphics used in the age before television needed some resourceful ideas. The graphic pamphlets and sales brochures handed out by sales people were works of art in themselves.

This page is from Mike Gleason, Herkimer, NY collection manuals and referance materials

The Universal Milking Machine Co.
Waukesha, Wisconsin
Started sales around 1925

Universal Natural

Universal Co-op

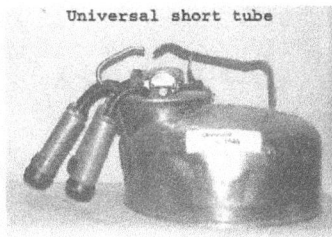
Universal short tube

These three Universal units are in my personal collection

Universal Milking Machine Manual and Graphics

In 1998 my wife Janet and I moved to the town of South Onondaga, NY. Living in Central NY and being a newly ordained UMC pastor, her first full time appointment was a 3 church situation. One of the parishioners at the S. Onondaga UMC was a dairy farmer/milking machine dealer named Harold Abbott. This was amazing to me for the fact that while I was in college (1971), my boss expanded the size of his dairy herd and built a free stall set up and milking parlor. We switched over from "Surge" buckets and dumping station to "Universal" milking parlor with weight jars. At that time, this was a radical change. Not that the Universal system was better than the Surge but it was cheaper. The dealer who sold and installed the Universal system was Harold Abbott.

So it was a surprise to me that at the same time I had become a resident in S.O., Mr. Abbott was cleaning out his father's basement of old useless milking machine parts and paper goods. He knew from previous visits that I was interested in old milker stuff. He was just putting it in the bucket of the tractor and going to take it to the farm dump and bury it. Yet for some reason he called me before he dumped this particular load. In that load were various milking machine parts and one 2 inch thick loose leaf binder full of advertising brochures and milking machine operator manuals from 1925 until early 1970's in excellent condition. All of the Information and the majority of milking machine parts of the Universal brand in my collection came from the one tractor bucket full of junk.

This page is from Mike Gleason, Herkimer, NY collection manuals and referance materials

Collector's Corner

While this book tries to speak to the larger role of milking machines in the history of the dairy industry, it never would've been written without the collection of Mike Gleason. This section provides some information about his collection of antique milkers and related literature. The story behind his own collection is perhaps best expressed in his own essay on the subject below:

Why Collect anything?

Collecting: a crazy topic? Yes it is. Many of us have an inherent need to possess something unuusal. It only has to catch your fancy, and you are on the road to somewhere for something.

My quest for milking machines and the knowledge about them began one summer day about 27 or 28 years ago (1980). I was the herdsperson on a dairy farm in Upstate NY. I grew up down by Labrador Hollow Unique Area. I had packed the wife and kids into the car (1978 Datsun B-210) and headed towards Herkimer to a gun museum (I don't own a gun, don't hunt, really have no use for a gun). Somewhere between here and there we stopped at a garage sale. Lo and behold what do I see, but a Perfection (circa 1916) milking machine lid and two tiny claws like I had never seen before. Well $10.00 later I packed it in the car and we were on our way for the rest of our vacation. This sat on my desk at home as a conversation piece (not much of one, really!), and it took me until the fall of 2005 to collect the rest of the machine.

The next piece collected about 1985 were 3 pulsators for an early 1950's McCormick-Deering milking machine. This was another gem of which I had never seen or heard of before. About 1986 while managing the Milking Parlor at the State Fair and talking with a farmer from western NY, I found out that they were still using McCormick-Deering milking machines at home. As the company was out of business they were always looking for extra parts. We made a swap, two of my pulsators for an extra pail and lid that they had. Another milking machine completed!

My milking machine collection now numbers about 63 units representing about 27 different brands.

Collecting milking machines leads to spotting other items related to the dairy industry: From tin signs (by milking machine brand) on the dining room wall to milk bottles lined up on shelves to early manuals for operation and service of said milking machines (over 4000 pages of fine reading). There is no sense having milking machines if you do not understand how they work and why they were designed to operate as they do. About the only way modern milking machines can change is in the computer chip that operates it.

Moral of this story is that collecting anything is addictive and very time consuming but also a lot of fun. Every time I come home with a new piece my wife will look at me with amusement and say, "Mike, you're out of control." Maybe I *am* out of control, but I have met a lot of good folks along the way with the same passion for collecting as I have. Maybe not "milking machines" but collecting **"whatever"**.

Here's another of Mike's amusing anecdotes about collecting:

On the Hunt for the Uebler Milker

One Saturday in early November 2007 I decided to take a trip to a friend's home in Morrisville, NY. After a couple hours of drinking coffee, I decided to visit a couple of milking machine dealers in the area. Neither dealer had anything I could use (old parts), but both had me leave my card and promised to call me if anything surfaced. I shrugged Okay to an average day collecting and went home. In the meantime when I got home, a piece I had placed a bid on had finished selling on Ebay, and I didn't get it. I was bummed. Two misses in one week. That's the way collecting goes sometimes. Five days later one of the dealers called and said that he had a lead for me. He asked me if I had I ever heard of the **Uebler** Milker? Well. I wasn't long in calling and finding out the "scoop." I found there was a retired dairyman's wife who had three Uebler Milkers for sale, and she lived in the town of Holland Patent, NY. He gave me her phone number and I called her right away. These units were her father's, which he had bought in 1940. She and her husband milked with them from 1947 until 1958 when they sold the cows. I made arrangements to meet her the next morning to look at them.

My wife and I headed out the next morning on a 60 mile road trip to Holland Patent. We drove into a neat farmstead and a lady came from the house to greet us. I introduced myself and Janet and started to look over the building and talk about their farming experience. About an hour later she took us to the milk house to see the elusive "Uebler" milking machine. Once I spied the milking machines, I knew that I was not leaving without buying all three. They were in near-perfect condition and still had the rubber pieces from the last time they milked a cow. The elusive "Uebler was found and in it's new home. The next journey is to find the owner's manual for this beast.

A road trip to find an owner's manual for **"Uebler"** Milking machines was on 11-26-07. The day began at 5:30 AM. With my first cup of coffee in hand, I went to the diner in Lafayette for breakfast and general bull shoot and was home by 7:30 AM. I went to the computer to find the address for Eastern Crown Inc., located in Vernon NY so that I could mapquest directions. I left home about 8:30 AM. After about an hour of travel I stopped at a Nice & Easy "stop and rob." After getting gas and another cup of coffee to go, I asked a couple of older gentlemen for final directions to my destination. As it turned out, I was only about 6 miles and two turns from where I wanted to be. I arrived at E.C.I. about 10:15. In talking with the parts man, I got the distinct feeling that he thought I had a screw loose for collecting old milking machines. I bought 2 sets of inflations for the **"Empire"** milking machine from late 1930's. And the parts man gave me another place I should stop and check for milking machine parts (an older established farm machinery dealership). This part of the trip found me backtracking about 15 miles to town of Munnsville, NY The owner of this dealership didn't have any manuals or parts on hand that he knew about, but he told me that his father had died a couple of months ago and that he had yet to go through his dad's basement which was full of old paper stuff from over the years. (Apparently his father had a hard time parting with old advertising pieces also.) He said if he found anything relating to old milking machines he would give me a call. After getting lost a couple more times I arrived home about 3:00 PM. A lot of road's traveled; no new milkers or manuals were found, but many nice people were met and hopefully some new pieces will be coming down the road in time. I left many "Mike's Milker" cards throughout Central NY.

Finding the Perfection Milker

After finding and completing my first Perfection unit I started going to one garage sale after another. As it turns out the aluminum milker pails all looked alike from one brand to another. A good reason for that they were all stamped on bottom, "Ware-ever Aluminum". <u>Ware-ever Aluminum Company</u> made them all. The only difference by brand was the difference of the lid circumference. The same idea seems to apply to the steel buckets. Apparently these were supplied to the milker companies as were the aluminums, but these had <u>Solar</u> stamped on the bottom.

In 1998 received my first computer, a gift from my son. While searching the internet one day I found EBAY. Here we go!!!!

The first pieces of milker stuff were the pulsator, claw, shells and inflations for the Perfection "Automatic" Milking Machine. Now I had the pail and some more parts, but I lacked the <u>lid </u>to complete another Perfection unit. In 2005 I was setting up a display of milkers at the NYS Fair, and one of the State Fair veterinarians stopped and asked if I would be interested in acquiring a few old milker parts that he had at home. Why not? I am always on the lookout for parts to complete a milker unit. I received the parts and they were 3 lids for the "automatic." It helped to complete this unit pictured. I sold the other lids on EBAY .They were bought by 2 grandsons of the inventor **Lauritz Dinesen .**

The coup de grace for this section is aimed toward other collectors of dairy memorabilia: it is an itemized list of the milkers & related paraphernalia in Mike's collection:

Collection Inventory as of Spring 2012

1-   AMERICAN COW MILKER

2-   ANDERSON PORTABLE MIKER 1940'S

2a-   AMERICAN FLYER 2 pges

2b.   Blue Ribbon Electric 7 pges

2c.   Colvin Hydraulic parlor 2 pgs

2d.   Clean-Easy Ben Anderson 2 pictures

3-   BURRELL B-L-K MILKER early 1920's

4-   Burrell-Lawrence-Kennedy Cow Milker small

5-   Trayeuse Mechanique B-L-K in French

5-a   Burrell – Directions for Burrell 18 pgs. 1918

5b.   Cascade 5 pges

6-   Conde Yellow color brochures 2

7-   Conde Milking Equipment "600" milker

7a.   DeGroff Simplicity Milker 1 16 pg flyer

8-   Empire letter May 29,1944

9-   Empire "Milks like a sucking calf" 1928

10-   Empire Milking Machine 1925

11-   Empire service manual 5-44

Inflation and shell guides

4-   Sta-rite "Crown Catalog D7011" 1970

5-   Conewango "Catalog 61-1" 1961(43 pgs)

6-   Conewango "Rubber parts and Supplies" 1949 21

DeLaval

68-Delaval Milker 1921

69-Delaval Milker Instructions 1919

70- Delaval "price list" 1939

71- Delaval Monthly 1930

72- Delaval Milker "controlled Milking" 1951

73- Delaval Handbook 1949

74- Delaval "Speedway suspended" 1957

75- Delaval New Suspended 1957

76- Delaval Model "F" combine

77- Delaval Parts List 152

78- Delaval "Sterling" Instruction

79- Delaval Speedway 1941

80- Delaval Sterling 1944

81- Delaval "Magnetic" Speedway 1954

82- Delaval "Model F" Combine Milker

83- Delaval "Yearbook" 1948 +1949

Appendix A: References & Attribution

American Milker	From an advertising flyer (1865)
Anderson Milker	From a 1930's advertising flyer
Ben Anderson	From a 1940's advertising flyer and pictures
Berry milker	From Dr. Paul Dettloff's book "Milking Machine Guide"
Baldwin, Anna	Ilustration From Dr. Paul Dettloff's book "Milking Machine Guide"
Blue Ribbon Electric	From a 1940's Advertising Flyer
Burrell Milker	Pages from 1920's Sales booklet
Burton-Page Milker	Taken from a 1930's Sales instruction flyer
B-V Milker	From Dr. Paul Dettloff's book "Milking Machine Guide"
Calf-way Milker	Illustration from Dr. Paul Dettloff's book "Milking Machine Guide"
Chore-boy Milker	From Dr. Paul Dettloff's Book "Milking Machine Guide"
Colvin Hydraulic	From Scientific American Magazine (1868)
Conde Milker	Illustrations are from Dr. Paul Dettloff's book
Conde Milker	Eearly 1960's Conde Advertising Flyer
Dairy Maid	Illustrations are from Dr. Paul Dettloff's Book "Milking Machine Guide"
Delaval	Assorted 1920's-1940's Delaval advertisement flyers and booklets
Disbrow	Illustrations are from Dr. Paul Dettloff's book "Milking Machine Guide"
Duplex	Illustrations are from advertising flyers in my collection
Empire	Illustrations are from "Empire" manuals and advertising flyers

EverReady	Illustrations are from 1930-1940 manuals
Fairbanks-Morse	Information is from a 1930's "Fairbanks-Morse manual
Fords	Information is from a 1927 advertising flyer
Galloway	Illustration is from Dr. Paul Dettloff's book "Milking Machine Guide"
Globe	Information is from a 1956 manual and advertising flyer
Hinman	Information is from 1915, 1921, and 1930 advertising flyers and manuals
Hoegger	Illustration is from Dr. Paul Dettloff's book "Milking Machine Guide"
Marlow	Information and illustrations are from advertising flyers
Montgomery-Wards	Information and illustrations are from manuals
Pinetree	Information and illustrations are from manual and advertisement flyers
Page	Information and illustrations are from manual
Perfection	Information is from early manuals and advertising flyers in my collection
Rite-Way	Information and illustrations are from manuals
Sears Prima	Information and illustrations are from manuals
Sears-Roebuck	Information and illustrations are from manuals
Sharples	Information and illustrations are from advertisement flyers (1912, 1914 and 1920)
Uebler	Information from an envelope
Universal	Information and illustrations are from manuals and advertisement flyers (1926-1950)
Westfalia	Information from the Westfalia-Surge company

www.ingramcontent.com/pod-product-compliance
Lightning Source LLC
Chambersburg PA
CBHW080532090426

42733CB00015B/2568